THE EMERGENCE
OF MODERN
EUROPE

POWER AND RELIGION IN MEDIEVAL AND RENAISSANCE TIMES

THE EMERGENCE OF MODERN EUROPE

EDITED BY KELLY ROSCOE

Britannica
Educational Publishing

IN ASSOCIATION WITH

ROSEN
EDUCATIONAL SERVICES

Published in 2018 by Britannica Educational Publishing (a trademark of Encyclopædia Britannica, Inc.) in association with The Rosen Publishing Group, Inc.
29 East 21st Street, New York, NY 10010

Distributed exclusively by Rosen Publishing.
To see additional Britannica Educational Publishing titles, go to rosenpublishing.com.

First Edition

Britannica Educational Publishing
J.E. Luebering: Executive Director, Core Editorial
Andrea R. Field: Managing Editor, Compton's by Britannica

Rosen Publishing
Meredith Day: Editor
Nelson Sá: Art Director
Brian Garvey: Designer
Cindy Reiman: Photography Manager
Bruce Donnola: Photo Researcher

Library of Congress Cataloging-in-Publication Data

Names: Roscoe, Kelly, editor.
Title: The emergence of modern Europe / edited by Kelly Roscoe.
Description: First edition. I New York : Britannica Educational Publishing, in association with Rosen Educational Services, 2018. I Series: Power and religion in medieval and renaissance times I Includes bibliographical references and index.
Identifiers: LCCN 2016053737 I ISBN 9781680486216 (library bound : alk. paper)
Subjects: LCSH: Europe--History--17th century. I History, Modern--17th century. I Thirty Years' War, 1618-1648.
Classification: LCC D246 .E47 2018 I DDC 940.2/2--dc23
LC record available at https://lccn.loc.gov/2016053737

Manufactured in China

Photo credits: Cover, pp. 3, 13, 43, 56, 72, 88, 105 Conde/Shutterstock.com; pp. 8-9, 106, 110 © Photos.com/Thinkstock; pp. 16-17 DEA/A. Dagli Orti/De Agostini/Getty Images; pp. 20-21, 22, 76-77 Print Collector/Hulton Archive/Getty Images; pp. 26-27 Print Collector/Hulton Fine Art Collection/Getty Images; p. 31 Universal History Archive/Universal Images Group/Getty Images; pp. 34-35, 52 De Agostini Picture Library/Getty Images; pp. 40-41 Universal Images Group/Getty Images; pp. 45, 64-65, 112, 114 Encyclopædia Britannica, Inc.; p. 47 Alamy Stock Photo; p. 49 Everett - Art/Shutterstoc.com; p. 58 Georgios Kollidas/Shutterstock.com; pp. 60, 74-75 ullstein bild/Getty Images; pp. 66-67 Apic/Hulton Archive/Getty Images; p. 69 Interfoto/Alamy Stock Photo; p. 80 Courtesy of the Kunsthistorisches Museum, Vienna; pp. 84-85 Christophe Boisvieux/Corbis Historical/Getty Images; pp. 90-91 Imagno/Hulton Fine Art Collection/Getty Images; p. 93 Courtesy of the Bayerische Staatsgemaldesammlungen, Munich; p. 94 Private Collection/Bridgeman Images; pp. 96-97 ZU_09/Getty Images; pp.102-103 Deutsches Historisches Museum, Berlin, Germany/© DHM/Bridgeman Images; interior pages background and border graphics Roberto Castillo/Shutterstock.com; back cover flourish Drakonova/Shutterstock.com

Contents

Introduction

In the 15th century, observers such as the philosopher and clerical statesman Nicholas of Cusa suggested that the "Middle Age" had attained its conclusion and a new era had begun. The Papacy, the symbol of the spiritual unity of Christendom, had lost much of its prestige in the Great Western Schism, a period from 1378 to 1417 in which there were two, and later three, rival popes. Lay ideals in the Italian peninsula also began to affect the Papacy. In the 16th century, the Protestant Reformation reacted against the worldliness and corruption of the Holy See, and the Roman Catholic church responded in its turn by a revival of piety known as the Counter-Reformation. While the forces that were to erupt in the Protestant movement were gathering strength, the narrow horizons of the Old World were widened by the expansion of Europe to America and the East.

The 16th century in Europe was a period of vigorous economic expansion. This expansion in turn played a major role in the many other transformations—social, political, and cultural—of the early modern age. By 1500 the population in most areas of Europe was increasing after two centuries of decline or stagnation. The bonds of commerce within

The Council of Constance took action to end the Great Western Schism, an event that contributed to the papacy losing some influence in the late Middle Ages.

Europe tightened. The great geographic discoveries then in process were integrating Europe into a world economic system. New commodities, many of them imported from recently discovered lands, enriched material life. Both trade and the production of goods increased as a result of new ways of organizing production. Merchants, entrepreneurs, and bankers accumulated and manipulated capital in unprecedented volume. Most historians locate in the 16th century the beginning, or at least the maturing, of Western capitalism. Capital assumed a major role not only in economic organization but also in political life and international relations. Culturally, new values—many of them associated with the Renaissance and Reformation—diffused through Europe and changed the ways in which people acted and the perspectives by which they viewed themselves and the world.

This world of early capitalism, however, can hardly be regarded as stable or uniformly prosperous. Financial crashes were common; the Spanish crown, the heaviest borrower in Europe, suffered repeated bankruptcies (in 1557, 1575–77, 1596, 1607, 1627, and 1647). The poor and destitute in society became, if not more numerous, at least more visible. Even as capitalism advanced in the West, the once-free peasants of central and eastern Europe slipped into serfdom. The apparent prosperity of the 16th century gave way in the middle and late periods of the 17th century to a "general crisis" in many European regions. Politically, the new centralized states insisted on new levels of cultural conformity on the part of their subjects. Several states expelled Jews, and almost all of them refused to tolerate religious dissenters. Culturally, in spite of the revival of ancient learning and the reform of the churches, a hysterical fear of witches grasped large segments of the population, including the learned. Understandably, historians have had difficulty defining the exact place of this complex century in the course of European development.

In western Europe, nation-states emerged under strong monarchical governments, breaking down local immunities and destroying the unity of the European *respublica Christiana* (Christian republic). Centralized bureaucracy came to replace medieval government. Underlying economic changes affected social stability. Secular values prevailed in politics, and the concept of a balance of power came to dominate international relations. Diplomacy and warfare were conducted by new methods. Sovereigns established permanent embassies in other states, and on the battlefield standing armies of professional and mercenary soldiers took the place of the feudal array that had reflected the social structure of the past. At the same time, scientific discoveries cast doubt on the traditional cosmology. The systems of

Aristotle and Ptolemy, which had long been sanctified by clerical approval, were undermined by Copernicus, Mercator, Galileo, and Kepler.

Religious, dynastic, territorial, and commercial rivalries among the states of Europe led to a series of wars known as the Thirty Years' War (1618–48). Its destructive campaigns and battles occurred over most of Europe, and, when it ended with the Treaty of Westphalia in 1648, the map of Europe had been irrevocably changed.

CHAPTER ONE

ECONOMICS AND SOCIETY

The 16th century's economic expansion owed much to powerful changes that were already under way by 1500. At that time, Europe comprised only between one-third and one-half the population it had possessed in about 1300. The infamous Black Death of 1347–50 principally accounts for the huge losses, but plagues were recurrent, famines frequent, wars incessant, and social tensions high as the Middle Ages ended. The late medieval disasters radically transformed the structures of European society—the ways by which it produced food and goods, distributed income, organized its society and state, and looked at the world.

The huge human losses altered the old balances among the classical "factors of production"—labour, land, and capital. The fall in population forced up wages in the towns and depressed rents in the countryside, as the fewer workers remaining could command a higher "scarcity value." In contrast, the costs of land and capital fell; both grew relatively more abundant and cheaper as human numbers shrank. Expensive labour and cheap land and capital encouraged "factor substitution," the replacement of the costly factor (labour) by the cheaper ones (land and capital). This substitution of land and capital for labour can be seen, for example, in the widespread conversions of arable land to pastures. A few shepherds, supplied with capital (sheep) and extensive pastures, could generate a higher return than plowland, intensively farmed by many well-paid labourers.

Capital could also support the technology required to develop new tools, enabling labourers to work more productively. The late Middle Ages was accordingly a period of significant technological advances linked with high capital investment in labour-saving devices. The development of printing by movable metal type substituted an expensive machine, the press, for many human copyists. Gunpowder and firearms gave smaller armies greater fighting power. Changes in shipbuilding and in the development of navigational aids allowed bigger ships to sail with smaller crews over longer distances. By 1500 Europe achieved what it had never possessed before: a technological edge over all other civilizations. Europe was thus equipped for worldwide expansion.

Social changes also were pervasive. With a falling population, the cost of basic foodstuffs (notably wheat) declined. With cheaper food, people in both countryside and city could use their higher earnings to diversify and improve their diets—to consume more meat, dairy products, and beverages. They also could afford more manufactured products from the towns, to the benefit of the urban economies.

The falling costs of the basic foodstuffs (cereals) and the continuing firm price of manufactures diverted income from countryside to town. The late medieval price movements thus favored urban artisans over peasants and merchants over landlords. Towns achieved a new weight in society; the number of towns counting more than 10,000 inhabitants increased from 125 in about 1300 to 154 in 1500, even as the total population was dropping. These changes undermined the leadership of the landholding nobility and enhanced the power and influence of the great merchants and bankers of the cities. The 16th would be a "bourgeois century."

Culturally, the disasters of the late Middle Ages had the effect of altering attitudes and in particular of undermining the medieval faith that speculative reason could master the secrets of the universe. In an age of ferocious and unpredictable epidemics, the accidental and the unexpected seemed to dominate the course of human affairs. In social life, there was evident a novel emphasis on close observation, on the need to study each changing situation to arrive at a basis for action.

The 16th century thus owed much to trends originating in the late Middle Ages, but new developments also shaped its achievements. Those developments affected population; money and prices; agriculture, trade, manufacturing, and banking; social and political institutions; and cultural attitudes.

DEMOGRAPHICS

For the continent as a whole, the population growth under way by 1500 continued over the "long" 16th century until the second or third decade of the 17th century. An estimate by the American historian Jan De Vries set Europe's population (excluding Russia and the Ottoman Empire) at 61.6 million in 1500, 70.2 million in 1550, and 78.0 million in 1600; it then lapsed back to 74.6 million in 1650. The distribution of population across the continent was also shifting. Northwestern Europe (especially the Low Countries and the British Isles) witnessed the most vigorous expansion; England's population more than doubled between 1500, when it stood at an estimated 2.6 million, and 1650, when it probably attained 5.6 million. Northwestern Europe also largely escaped the demographic downturn of the mid-17th century, which was especially pronounced in Germany, Italy, and Spain. In Germany, the Thirty Years' War (1618–48) may have cost the country, according to different estimates, between 25 and 40 percent of its population.

Cities also grew, though slowly at first. The proportion of Europeans living in cities with 10,000 or more residents increased from 5.6 percent of the total population in 1500 to only 6.3 percent in 1550. The towns of England continued to suffer a kind of depression, now often called "urban decay," in the first half of the century. The process of urbanization then accelerated, placing 7.6 percent of the population in cities by 1600, and even continued during the 17th-century crisis. The proportion of the population in cities of more than 10,000 inhabitants reached 8.3 percent in 1650.

More remarkable than the slow growth in the number of urban residents was the formation of cities of a size never achieved in the medieval period. These large cities

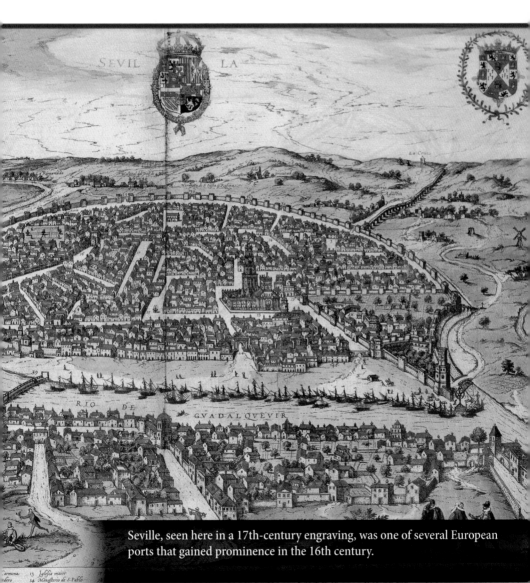

Seville, seen here in a 17th-century engraving, was one of several European ports that gained prominence in the 16th century.

were of two principal types. Capitals and administrative centres—such as Naples, Rome, Madrid, Paris, Vienna, and Moscow—give testimony to the new powers of the state and its ability to mobilize society's resources in support of courts and bureaucracies. Naples, one of Europe's largest cities in 1550, was also one of its poorest.

Commercial ports, which might also have been capitals, formed a second set of large cities: examples include Venice, Livorno, Sevilla (Seville), Lisbon, Antwerp, Amsterdam, London, Bremen, and Hamburg. About 1550, Antwerp was the chief port of the north. In 1510, the Portuguese moved their trading station from Brugge to Antwerp, making it the chief northern market for the spices they were importing from India. The Antwerp bourse, or exchange, simultaneously became the leading money market of the north. At its heyday in mid-century, the city counted 90,000 inhabitants. The revolt of the Low Countries against Spanish rule (from 1568) ruined Antwerp's prosperity. Amsterdam, which replaced it as the greatest northern port, grew from 30,000 in 1550 to 65,000 in 1600 and 175,000 in 1650. The mid-17th century—a period of recession in many European regions—was Holland's golden age. Late in the century, Amsterdam faced the growing challenge of another northern port, which was also the capital of a powerful national state—London. With 400,000 residents by 1650 and growing rapidly, London then ranked below only Paris (440,000) as Europe's largest city. Urban concentrations of such magnitude were unprecedented; in the Middle Ages, the largest size attained was roughly 220,000, in Paris about 1328.

Another novelty of the 16th century was the appearance of urban systems, or hierarchies of cities linked together by their political or commercial functions. Most European cities had been founded in medieval or even in ancient times, but they long remained intensely competitive, duplicated each other's functions, and never coalesced during the Middle Ages into tight urban systems. The more intensive, more far-flung commerce of the early modern age required a clearer distribution of functions and cooperation as much as competition. The centralization of governments in the 16th century also demanded clearly defined lines of authority and firm divisions of functions between national and regional capitals.

TRADE AND THE "ATLANTIC REVOLUTION"

The new importance of northwestern Europe in terms of overall population and concentration of large cities reflects in part the "Atlantic revolution," the redirection of trade routes brought about by the great geographic discoveries. The Atlantic revolution, however, did not so much replace the old lines of medieval commerce as build upon them. In the Middle Ages, Italian ports—Venice and Genoa in particular—dominated trade with the Middle East and supplied Europe with Eastern wares and spices. In the north, German cities, organized into a loose federation known as the Hanseatic League, similarly dominated Baltic trade. When the Portuguese in 1498 opened direct maritime links with India, Venice faced the competition of the Atlantic ports, first Lisbon and Antwerp. Nonetheless, Venice effectively responded to the new competition and attained in the 16th century its height of commercial importance. Genoa was not well placed to take advantage of the Atlantic discoveries, but Genoese bankers played a central role in the finances of Spain's overseas empire and in its military ventures in Europe. Italians did not quickly relinquish the prominence as merchants and bankers that had distinguished them in the Middle Ages.

In the north, the Hanseatic towns faced intensified competition from the Dutch, who from about 1580 introduced a new ship design (the *fluitschip*, a sturdy, cheaply built cargo vessel) and new techniques of shipbuilding, including wind-powered saws. Freight charges dropped and the size of the Dutch merchant marine soared; by the mid-17th century, it probably exceeded in number of vessels all the other mercantile fleets of Europe combined. The English competed for a share in the Baltic trade, though they long remained well behind the Dutch.

In absolute terms, Baltic trade was booming. In 1497 the ships passing through the Sound separating Denmark from Sweden numbered 795; 100 years later the number registered by the toll collectors reached 6,673. The percentage represented by Hanseatic ships rose over the same century from roughly 20 to 23–25 percent; the Germans were not yet routed from these eastern waters.

In terms of maritime trade, the Atlantic revolution may well have stimulated rather than injured the older exchanges. At the same time, new competition from the western ports left both Hanseatics and Italians vulnerable to the economic downturn of the 17th century. For both the

1520 Antwerp

The port of Antwerp became one of Europe's greatest industrial, financial, and cultural centres in the 16th century.

Hanseatic and Italian cities, the 17th—and not the 16th—century was the age of decline. At Lübeck in 1628, at the last meeting of the Hanseatic towns, only 11 cities were represented, and later attempts to call a general meeting ended in failure.

This illustration from a 1556 book about metalwork depicts the tools and processes of a silver refinery.

PRICES AND INFLATION

Changes in price levels in the 16th century profoundly affected every economic sector, but in ways that are disputed. The period witnessed a general inflation, known traditionally as the "price revolution." It was rooted in part in frequent monetary debasements; the French kings, for example, debased or altered their chief coinage, the *livre tournois*, in 1519, 1532, 1549, 1561, 1571–75 (four mutations), and 1577. Probably more significant (though even this is questioned) was the infusion of new stocks of precious metal, especially silver, into the money supply. The medieval economy had suffered from a chronic shortage of precious metals. From the late 15th century, however, silver output, especially from German mines, increased and remained high through the 1530s. New techniques of sinking and draining shafts, extracting ore, and refining silver made mining a booming industry. From 1550 "American treasure," chiefly from the great silver mine at Potosí in Peru (now in Bolivia), arrived in huge volumes in Spain, and from Spain it flowed to the many European regions where Spain had significant military or political engagements. Experts estimate (albeit on shaky grounds) that the stock of monetized silver increased by three or three and a half times during the 16th century.

At the same time, the growing numbers of people who had to be fed, clothed, and housed assured that coins would circulate rapidly. In monetary theory, the level of prices varies directly with the volume of money and the velocity of its circulation. New sources of silver and new numbers of people thus launched (or at least reinforced) pervasive inflation. According to one calculation, prices rose during the century in nominal terms by a factor of six and in real terms by a factor of three. The rate is low by modern standards, but it struck a society accustomed to stability. Inflation contributed no small part to the period's social tensions.

On the other hand, the price revolution certainly stimulated the economy. It clearly penalized the inactive. Those who wished to do no more than maintain their traditional standard of living had, nonetheless, to assume an active economic stance. The increased supply of money seems further to have lowered interest rates—another advantage for the entrepreneur. The price revolution by itself did not assure capital accumulation and the birth of capitalism, but it did bring about increased outlays of entrepreneurial energy.

LANDLORDS AND PEASANTS

The growing population in the 16th century and the larger concentrations of urban dwellers required abundant supplies of food. Money again flowed into the countryside to pay for food, especially wheat. But the social repercussions of the rising price of wheat varied in the different European regions.

In eastern Germany (with the exception of electoral Saxony), Poland, Bohemia, Hungary, Lithuania, and even eventually Russia, the crucial change was the formation of a new type of great property, called traditionally in the German literature the *Gutsherrschaft* (ownership of an estate). The estate was divided into two principal parts: the landlord's demesne, from which he took all the harvest, and the farms of the peasants, who supplied the labour needed to work the demesne. The peasants (and their children after them) were legally serfs, bound to the soil. These bipartite, serf-run estates superficially resemble the classic manors of the early Middle Ages but differ from them in that the new estates were producing primarily for commercial markets. The binding of the peasants of eastern Europe to the soil and the imposition of heavy labour services constitute, in another traditional term, the "second serfdom."

In the contemporary west (and in the east before the 16th century), the characteristic form of great property was the *Grundherrschaft* ("ownership of land"). This was an aggregation of rent-paying properties. The lord might also be a cultivator, but he worked his land through hired labourers.

What explains the formation of the *Gutsherrschaft* in early modern eastern Europe? The nobility and gentry, even without planning to do so, accumulated large tracts of abandoned land during the late medieval population collapse. As competition for their labour remained high, peasants were prone to move from one estate to another, in search of better terms. Moreover, the landlords had little capital to hire salaried hands and, in the largely rural east, there were few sources of capital. They had, however, one recourse. They dominated the weak governments of the region, and even a comparatively strong ruler, like the Russian tsar, wished to accommodate the demands of the gentry. In 1497 the Polish gentry won the right to export their grain without paying duty. Further legislation bound the peasants to the soil and obligated them to work the lord's demesne. The second serfdom gradually spread over eastern Europe; it was established in Poland as early as 1520; in Russia it was legally imposed in the Ulozhenie (Law Code) of 1649. At least in Poland, the western market for cereals was a principal factor in reviving serfdom, a seemingly primitive form of labour organization.

No second serfdom developed in western Europe, even though the stimulus of high wheat prices was equally powerful. Harassed landlords, pressed to raise their revenues, had more options than their eastern counterparts. They might look to a profession or even a trade or, more commonly, seek at court an appointment paying a salary or a pension.

The western princes did not want local magnates to dominate their communities, as this would erode their own authority. They consequently defended the peasants against the encroachments of the gentry. Finally, landlords in the west could readily find capital. They could use the money either to hire workers or to improve their leased properties, in expectation of gaining higher rents. The availability of capital in the west and its scarcity in the east were probably the chief reasons why the agrarian institutions of eastern and western Europe diverged so dramatically in the 16th century.

The 16th century witnessed a conversion—widespread though never complete—from systems of feudal to capitalist rents. The late medieval population collapse increased the mobility of the peasant population; a peasant who settled for one year and one day in a "free village" or town received perpetual immunity from personal charges. Personal dues thus eroded rapidly; dues weighing upon the land persisted longer but could not be raised. It was therefore in the landlord's interest to convert feudal tenures into leaseholds, and this required capital.

In England upon the former manors, farmers (the original meaning of the term was leaseholder or rent payer), who held land under long-term leases, gradually replaced

Dutch painter Pieter Bruegel the Elder portrayed peasants hard at work in the fields in *The Harvesters* in 1565.

copyholders, or tenants subject only to feudal dues. These farmers constituted the free English yeomanry, and their appearance marks the demise of the last vestiges of medieval serfdom. In the Low Countries, urban investors bought up the valuable lands near towns and converted them into leaseholds, which were leased for high rents over long terms. The heavy infusions of urban capital into Low Country agriculture helped make it technically the most advanced in Europe, a model for improving landlords elsewhere. In central and southern France and in central Italy, urban investment in the land was closely linked to a special type of sharecropping lease, called the *métayage* in France and the *mezzadria* in Italy. The landlord (typically a wealthy townsman) purchased plots, consolidated them into a farm, built a house upon it, and rented it. Often, he also provided the implements needed to work the land, livestock, and fertilizer. The tenant gave as rent half of the harvest. The spread of this type of sharecropping in the vicinity of towns had begun in the late Middle Ages and was carried vigorously forward in the 16th century. Nonetheless, the older forms of feudal tenure, and even some personal charges, also persisted, especially in Europe's remote and poorer regions. The early modern countryside presents an infinitely complex mixture of old and new ways of holding and working the land.

Two further changes in the countryside are worth noting. In adopting Protestantism, the North German states, Holland, the Scandinavian countries, and England confiscated and sold, in whole or in part, ecclesiastical properties. Sweden, for example, did so in 1526–27, England in 1534–36. It is difficult to assess the exact economic repercussions of these secularizations, but the placing of numerous properties upon the land market almost surely encouraged the infusion of capital into (and the spread of capitalist forms of agrarian organization in) the countryside.

Second, the high price of wheat did not everywhere make cereal cultivation the most remunerative use of the land. The price of wool continued to be buoyant, and this, linked with the availability of cheap wheat from the east, sustained the conversion of plowland into pastures that also had begun in the late Middle Ages. In England this movement is called "enclosure." To many outspoken observers, clergy and humanists in particular, enclosures were destroying villages, uprooting the rural population, and multiplying beggars on the road and paupers in the towns.

In Spain, sheep and people also entered into destructive competition. Since the 13th century, sheepherding had fallen under the control of a guild known as the Mesta that was dominated by a few grandees. The Mesta practiced transhumance (alternation of winter and spring pastures); the flocks themselves moved seasonally along great trailways called *cañadas*. The government, which collected a tax on exported wool, was anxious to raise output and favoured the Mesta with many privileges. Cultivators along the cañadas were forbidden to fence their fields, lest the barriers impede the migrating sheep. Moreover, the government imposed ceiling prices on wheat in 1539. Damage from the flocks and the low price of wheat eventually crippled cereal cultivation, provoked widespread desertion of the countryside and overall population decline, and was a significant factor in Spain's 17th-century decline. High cereal prices primarily benefited not the peasants but the landlords. The landlords in turn spent their increased revenues on the amenities and luxuries supplied by towns. In spite of high food costs, town economies fared well.

PROTOINDUSTRIALIZATION

Historians favour the term "protoindustrialization" to describe the form of industrial organization that emerged

BANKING AND FINANCE

Perhaps the most spectacular changes in the 16th-century economy were in the fields of international banking and finance. Medieval bankers such as the Florentine Bardi and Peruzzi in the 14th century and the Medici in the 15th had operated on an international scale, but the full development of an international money market with supporting institutions did not develop until the 16th century. Its earliest architects were South German banking houses, from Augsburg and Nürnberg in particular, which were well situated to serve as financial intermediaries between such southern capitals as Rome (or commercial centres such as Venice) and the northern financial centre at Antwerp. Through letters of exchange drawn on the various bourses that were growing throughout Europe, these bankers were able to mobilize capital in fabulous amounts. In 1519 Jakob II Fugger the Rich of Augsburg amassed nearly two million florins for the Habsburg king of Spain, Charles I, who used the money to bribe the imperial electors (he was successfully elected Holy Roman emperor as Charles V). Money was shaping the politics of Europe.

The subsequent bankruptcies of the Spanish crown injured the German bankers; from 1580 or even earlier, the Genoese became the chief financiers of the Spanish government and empire. Through the central fair at Lyon and through letters of exchange and a complex variant known as the *asiento*, the Genoese transferred great sums from Spain to the Low Countries to pay the soldiers of the Spanish armies. In the mid-16th century, dissatisfied with Lyon, the Genoese set up a fictional fair, known as Bisenzone (Besançon), as a centre of their fiscal operations. Changing sites several times, "Bisenzone" from 1579 settled at Piacenza in Italy.

Bankers in the 16th century kept track of transactions between states across Europe, a system that presaged the modern institutions of international finance.

in the 16th century. The word was initially applied to cottage industries in the countryside. In spite of the opposition of urban guilds, rural residents were performing many industrial tasks. Agricultural labour did not occupy the peasants during the entire year, and they devoted their free hours to such activities as spinning wool or weaving and washing cloth. Peasants usually worked for lower remuneration than urban artisans. Protoindustrialization gave rural residents supplementary income, which conferred a certain immunity from harvest failures; it enabled them to marry younger and rear larger families; it prepared them, socially and psychologically, for eventual industrialization. The efforts of urban guilds to limit rural work enjoyed only limited success; in England, for example, the restrictions seem rarely to have been enforced. Cottage industries certainly existed in the Middle Ages, but the economic expansion of the 16th century diffused them over much larger areas of the European countryside, perhaps most visibly in England and western Germany.

More recently, historians have stressed the role of towns in this early form of industrial organization. Towns remained the centres from which the raw materials were distributed in the countryside. Moreover, urban entrepreneurs coordinated the efforts of the rural workers and marketed their finished products. Certain processes—usually the most highly skilled and the most remunerative—remained centred in cities. The principal achievement of 16th-century industry was not only the extension of industry into rural areas but also the greater integration of city and countryside.

This manner of organizing manufactures is known as the "putting-out system," an awkward translation of the

German *Verlagssystem*. The key to its operation was the entrepreneur, who purchased the raw materials, distributed them among the working families, passed the semifinished products from one artisan to another, and marketed the finished products. He was typically a great merchant resident in the town. As trade routes grew longer, the small artisan was placed at ever-greater distances from sources of supply and from markets. Typically, the small artisan would not have the knowledge of distant markets or of the preferences of distant purchasers and rarely had the money to purchase needed raw materials. The size of the trading networks and the volume of merchandise moving within them made the services of the entrepreneur indispensable and subordinated the workers to his authority.

The production of fabric remained the chief European industry, but two developments, both of them continuations of medieval changes, are noteworthy. In southern Europe the making of silk cloth, stimulated by the luxurious tastes of the age, gained unprecedented prominence. Lucca, Bologna, and Venice in Italy and Sevilla and Granada in Spain gained flourishing industries. Even more spectacular in its rise as a centre of silk manufacture was the city and region of Lyon in central France. Lyon was also a principal fair town, where goods of northern and southern Europe were exchanged. It was ideally placed to obtain silk cocoons or thread from the south and to market the finished cloth to northern purchasers. The silk industry is also notable in that most of the workers it employed were women.

Northern industry continued to concentrate on woolens but partially turned its efforts to producing a new type of cloth, worsteds. Worsteds were lighter and cheaper to make than woolens and did not require the services of a mill, which might have to be located near running water. Under the name of "new draperies," worsteds had come to dominate the Flemish wool industry in the late Middle Ages. In the 16th century, several factors—the growth of population and of markets, the revolt of the Low Countries against Spain, and religious persecutions, which led many skilled Protestant workers to seek refuge among their coreligionists—stimulated the worsted industry in England. England had developed a vigorous woolens industry in the late Middle Ages, and the spread of worsted manufacture made it a European leader in fabric production.

Another major innovation in 16th-century industrial history was the growing use of coal as fuel. England, with rich coal

This 16th-century engraving depicts the silk-making industry, which flourished in Europe for many centuries, especially in the Italian city-states and (from 1480) in France.

mines located close to the sea, could take particular advantage of this cheap mineral fuel. The port of Newcastle in Northumbria emerged in the 16th century as a principal supplier of coal to London consumers. As yet, coal could not be used for the direct smelting of iron, but it found wide application in glassmaking, brick baking, brewing, and the heating of homes. The use of coal eased the demand on England's rapidly diminishing forests and contributed to the growth of a coal technology that would make a crucial contribution to the later Industrial Revolution.

In industry, the 16th century was not so much an age of dramatic technological departures; rather, it witnessed the steady improvement of older technological traditions—in shipbuilding, mining and metallurgy, glassmaking, silk production, clock and instrument making, firearms, and others. Europe slowly widened its technological edge over non-European civilizations. Most economic historians further believe that protoindustrialization, and the commerce that supplied and sustained it, best explains the early accumulations of capital and the birth of a capitalist economy.

POLITICAL AND CULTURAL INFLUENCES ON THE ECONOMY

The centralized state of the early modern age exerted a decisive influence on the development of financial institutions and in other economic sectors as well. To maintain its power both within its borders and within the international system, the state supported a large royal or princely court, a bureaucracy, and an army. It was the major purchaser of weapons and war matériel. Its authority affected class balances. Over the century's course, the prince expanded his authority to make appointments and grant pensions. His control of resources softened the divisions among classes and facilitated social mobility. Several great merchants and bankers, the Fuggers among them, eventually were ennobled. Yet, in spending huge sums on war, the early modern state may also have injured the economy. The floating debt of the French crown came close to 10 million ecus (the ecu was worth slightly less than a gold florin), that of the Spanish, 20 million. These sums probably equaled the worth of the circulating coin in the two kingdoms. Only in England did the public debt remain at relatively modest proportions, about 200,000 gold ducats. Governments, with the exception of the English, were absorbing a huge part of the national wealth. The Spanish bankruptcies were also sure proof that Spain had insufficient resources to realize its ambitious imperial goals.

The effort to control the economy in the interest of enhancing state power is the essence of the political philosophy known as mercantilism. Many of the policies of 16th-century states affecting trade, manufactures, or money can be regarded as mercantilistic, but as yet they did not represent a coherent economic theory. The true age of mercantilism postdates 1650.

Cultural changes also worked to legitimize, even to inspire, the early modern spirit of enterprise. Many movements contributed to a reassessment of the mercantile or business life, and the rival religious confessions influenced one another. In the 17th century Calvinism viewed commercial success as a sign of God's favour, but 16th-century Roman Catholic scholastics (as the humanists before them) had come to regard the operations of the marketplace as natural; it was good for the merchant to participate in them. Martin Luther, in emphasizing that every Christian had received a calling (*Berufung*) from God, gave new dignity to all secular employments. Roman Catholics developed their own theory of the "vocation" to both secular and religious callings in what was a close imitation of the Lutheran *Berufung*.

A NEW SOCIAL HISTORY

The common people of Europe also experienced changes during this period. In particular, the role of women, nonconformists, and minorities provide a different look at how society functioned in early modern Europe.

Two fundamental changes affected the status of early modern women. Women under protoindustrialization were valued domestic workers, but they also had little economic independence: the male head of the household, the father or husband, gained the chief fruits of their labour. A second change, perhaps related to the first, was the advancing age of first marriage for women. Medieval girls were very young at first marriage, barely past puberty; these young girls were given to mature grooms who were in their middle or late 20s. By the late 16th century, parish marriage registers show that brides were nearly the same age as their grooms and both were mature persons, usually in their middle 20s. This is, in effect, what demographers call the modern, western European marriage pattern. Comparatively late ages at first marriage also indicate that significant numbers of both men and women would not marry at all.

Though the origins of this pattern remain obscure, it may be that families, recognizing the economic value of daughters, were anxious to retain their services as long as possible. European marriages were overwhelmingly patrilocal—that is, the bride almost always joined her husband's household. The near equality of ages between the marriage partners at least opened the possibility that the two would become true friends as well as spouses; this was harder to achieve when brides were young girls and their husbands mature and experienced.

The established religions of Europe, both Roman Catholic and Protestant, zealously sought to assure uniformity of belief in the regions they dominated. The courts inspired by them actively pursued not only the heterodox but also witches, the insane, and anyone who maintained an unusual style of life. The special papal court known as the Inquisition operated in many (though not all) Catholic states. Its judges carefully interrogated witnesses and kept good records. These records permit rare views into the depths of early modern society. They show how widespread was the belief in magic and the practice of witchcraft and how far popular culture diverged from the officially sanctioned ideologies.

Witches were hunted in the 16th century with a relentlessness never seen before, and it is difficult to determine why. Terrorized witnesses tended to respond in ways they thought would please their interrogators; thus, they reinforced stereotypes rather than revealing what they truly believed or did. Court records of this kind are not flawless sources, but they remain a rich vein of cultural history.

The 16th century also witnessed a continuing deterioration in the status of western Jews. They had been expelled from England in 1290 and from France in 1306 (the first of several expulsions and readmissions). Riots and killings accompanying the Black Death (the Jews were accused of poisoning the wells) had pushed the centres of German Jewry (the Ashkenazim) to the east, into Poland, Lithuania, and, eventually, the Russian Empire. In 1492 the Jews of Spain (the Sephardim), who had formed the largest and most culturally accomplished western community, were given the choice of conversion or expulsion. Many chose to leave for Portugal (from which they would also be subsequently expelled), the Low Countries, Italy, or the Ottoman Empire. Those who remained and ostensibly converted were called "New Christians," or Marranos, and many of these later chose to emigrate to more hospitable lands. Many Marranos continued to live as Jews while professing Christianity; accusations against them were commonly heard by the Inquisition in both Spain and Italy. Their position was especially distressing. Often, both Jews and Christians rejected them, the former for their ostensible conversion, the latter for secretly practicing Judaism.

The communities of exiles had different experiences. Jews in Holland made a major contribution to the country's great prosperity. The Italian states, papal Rome included, accepted the exiles, hoping to profit from their commercial and financial expertise. Yet the Jews were also subject to increasingly severe restrictions. The Jewish community at Venice, which absorbed large numbers of Iberian Jews and Marranos, formed the first ghetto (the word itself is Venetian, first used in 1516). The practice of confining Jews into walled quarters, locked at night, became the common social practice of early mod-

Suspected witches were often executed by burning or hanging. Three-fourths of European witch hunts occurred in western Germany, the Low Countries, France, northern Italy, and Switzerland.

ern states, at least in the central and eastern parts of the continent. The Sephardim, who continued to speak a form of Spanish known as Ladino, established large and prosperous colonies in Ottoman cities—Salonika, Istanbul, and Cairo among them. On balance, however, the early modern period in Europe was socially and culturally a dark age for Jewry.

During the early modern period, the western monarchies overcame much of the political localism of the medieval world and set a model that even divided Italy and Germany would eventually emulate. Economic integration advanced even more rapidly; markets in foodstuffs, spices, luxuries, and money extended throughout the continent: The skilled banker could marshal funds from all the continent's money markets; silks from Lucca were sold in Poland. Cities formed into hierarchies, still on a regional basis but surpassing in their effectiveness the loose associations of medieval urban places. Competition among the centralized states often led to destructive wars and terrible waste of resources; and the quest for unity brought shameful persecution upon those who could not or would not conform to the dominant culture.

CHAPTER TWO

THE STATE OF EUROPEAN POLITICS

uring this period, the European states developed into dynastic monarchies that established internal unification and abolished local privileges. Strong leaders such as Charles V of the Holy Roman Empire and Süleyman I the Magnificent of the Ottoman Empire dominated their states, though the aristocracy retained more influence in eastern Europe. Political nationalism was also reflected in the new states' exploration overseas in search of new trade routes.

NATION-STATES AND DYNASTIC RIVALRIES

In Spain the union of Aragon, Valencia, and Catalonia under John II of Aragon was extended to association with Castile through the marriage of his son Ferdinand with the Castilian heiress Isabella. The alliance grew toward union after the accession of the two sovereigns to their thrones in 1479 and

EXPLORATION OF THE NEW WORLD

Explorers in southwestern Europe began to seek new trade routes because the known trade routes were dominated by other powers. Access to the eastern Mediterranean Sea was barred by the fleets of Byzantium (the Seljuq Turks) and after 1453 by those of the Ottoman Turks. The other known trade routes from Europe were monopolized by Venice and Genoa (now in Italy). Portugal and Spain thus looked southward and westward for trade connections and riches.

In the last years of the 15th century, Portuguese navigators established the sea route to India and within a decade had secured control of the trade routes in the Indian Ocean and its approaches. Aside from trade, they were also motivated by scientific curiosity and the desire to convert indigenous peoples to Christianity. Similar hopes inspired Spanish exploitation of the discovery by Christopher Columbus of the Caribbean outposts of the American continent in 1492. The Treaties of Tordesillas and Saragossa in 1494 and 1529 split territory between the two powers, giving Spain most of what is now South America and granting Portuguese influence over Asia.

By the time of the Treaty of Saragossa, when Portugal secured the exclusion of Spain from the East Indies, Spain had begun the conquest of Central and South America. In 1519, the year in which Ferdinand Magellan embarked on the westward circumnavigation of the globe, Hernán Cortés launched his expedition against Mexico. The seizure of Peru by Francisco Pizarro and the enforcement of Portuguese claims to Brazil completed the major steps in the Iberian occupation of the continent. By the middle of the century, the age of the conquistadores was replaced by an era of colonization, based both on the procurement of precious metal by Indian labour and on pastoral and plantation economies using imported African slaves. The influx of bullion into Europe became significant in the late 1520s, and from about 1550 it began to produce a profound effect upon the economy of the Old World.

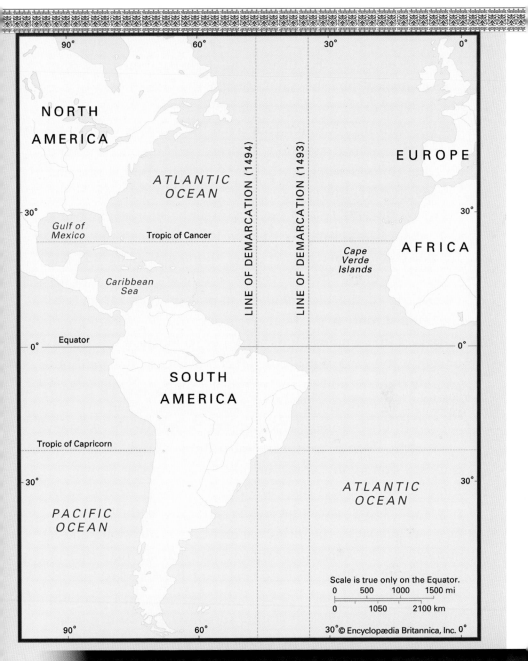

The division between Spanish territory (west of the line) and Portuguese territory (east of the line) was first defined by Pope Alexander VI (1493) and later revised by the Treaty of Tordesillas (1494).

1474, respectively. Ferdinand and Isabella then took joint action against the Moors of Granada, the French in Italy, and the independent kingdom of Navarre. Yet, at the same time, provincial institutions long survived the dynastic union, and the representative assembly (Cortes) of Aragon continued to cling to its privileges when its Castilian counterpart had ceased to play any effective part. Castilian interest in the New World and Aragonese ties in Italy, moreover, meant that Spain was constantly shifting focus between the Atlantic and the Mediterranean. The monarchy increased the central power by the absorption of military orders and the adaptation of the Hermandad, or police organization, and the Inquisition for political purposes. During the reign of Charles I (the emperor Charles V) centralization was quickened by the importation of Burgundian conciliar methods of government, and in the reign of Philip II, Spain was in practice an autocracy.

Other European monarchies imitated the system devised by Roman-law jurists and administrators in the Burgundian dominions along the eastern borders of France. In England and France, the Hundred Years' War (conventionally 1337–1453) had reduced the strength of the aristocracies, which were the principal opponents of monarchical authority. The Tudors in England pursued strong, efficient government, following the example of their Yorkist predecessors. Louis XI and Francis I did the same in France. In both countries revision of the administrative and judicial system proceeded through conciliar institutions, although in neither case did it result in the unification of different systems of law. A rising class of professional administrators came to fulfill the role of the king's executive. The creation of a

Thomas Cromwell was Henry VIII's principal adviser from 1532 to 1540, during which time he strengthened the royal administration.

central treasury under Francis I brought an order into French finances already achieved in England through Henry VII's adaptation of the machinery of the royal household. Henry VIII's minister, Thomas Cromwell, introduced an aspect of modernity into English fiscal administration by the creation of courts of revenue on bureaucratic lines. In both countries, the monarchy extended its influence over the government of the church. The unrestricted ability to make law was established by the English crown in partnership with Parliament.

In France the representative Estates-General lost its authority, and sovereignty reposed in the king in council. Supreme courts (*parlements*) possessing the right to register royal edicts imposed a slight and ineffective limitation on the absolutism of the Valois kings. The most able exponent of the reform of the judicial machinery of the French monarch was Charles IX's chancellor, Michel de L'Hôpital. He attempted to reform the judiciary in the 1560s, but his efforts were frustrated by the anarchy of the religious wars. In France the middle class aspired to ennoblement in the royal administration and mortgaged their future to the monarchy by investment in office and the royal finances. In England, on the other hand, a greater flexibility in social relations was preserved, and the middle class engaged in bolder commercial and industrial ventures.

CHARLES V

Territorial unity under the French crown was attained through the recovery of feudal land grants and, as in Spain, through marriage alliances. Brittany was regained in this way, although the first of the three Valois marriages with

Charles V inherited a Spanish and Habsburg empire extending across Europe, but he struggled to hold it together against the growing forces of Protestantism. He abdicated in 1556.

Breton heiresses also set in train the dynastic rivalry of Valois and Habsburg. When Charles VIII of France married Anne of Brittany, he stole the bride of the Austrian archduke and future emperor Maximilian I and also broke his own engagement to Margaret of Austria, Maximilian's daughter by Mary of Burgundy. Margaret's brother Philip, however, married Joan, heiress of Castile and Aragon, so that their son eventually inherited not only Habsburg Germany and the Burgundian Netherlands but also Spain, Spanish Italy, and America. The dominions of Charles V thus encircled France and incorporated the wealth of Spain overseas. Even after the division of this vast inheritance between his son, Philip II of Spain, and his brother, the emperor Ferdinand I, the conflict between the Habsburgs and the French crown dominated the diplomacy of Europe for more than a century.

The principal dynastic conflict of the age was less unequal than it seemed, for the greater resources of Charles V were offset by their disunity and by local independence. In the Low Countries he was able to complete the Seventeen Provinces by new acquisitions, but, although the coordinating machinery of the Burgundian dukes remained in formal existence, Charles's regents were obliged to respect local privileges and to act through constitutional forms. In Germany, where his grandfather Maximilian I had unsuccessfully tried to reform the constitution of the Holy Roman Empire, Charles V could do little to overcome the independence of the lay and ecclesiastical princes, the imperial knights, and the free cities. The revolts of the knights (1522) and the peasantry (1525), together with the political disaggregation imposed by the Reformation, rendered the empire a source of weakness.

Even in Spain, where the rebellion of the *comuneros* took place in 1520–21, his authority was sometimes flouted. His allies, England and the papacy, at times supported France to procure their own profit. France, for its part, possessed the advantages of internal lines of communication and a relatively compact territory, while its alliance with the Ottoman Empire maintained pressure on the Habsburg defenses in southeast Europe and the Mediterranean. Francis I, however, like his predecessors Charles VIII and Louis XII, made the strategic error of wasting his strength in Italy, where the major campaigns were fought in the first half of the century. Only under Henry II was it appreciated that the most suitable area for French expansion lay toward the Rhine.

THE OTTOMAN EMPIRE

A contemporary who rivaled the power and prestige of Francis I and Charles V was the ruler of the Ottoman Empire, the sultan Süleyman I the Magnificent (1520–66). With their infantry corps d'élite (the Janissaries), their artillery, and their cavalry, or *sipahi*s, the Ottomans were the foremost military power in Europe. Luckily for the Christian powers of Europe, the Ottomans were preoccupied by other concerns to their east, such as the Safavids, a powerful military order in Persia.

Süleyman overran Iraq and even challenged Portuguese dominion of the Indian Ocean from his bases in Suez and Basra. The Crimean Tatars acknowledged his rule, as did the corsair powers of Algiers, Tunis, and Tripoli. His armies conquered Hungary in 1526 and threatened Vienna in 1529.

The Ottoman victory in the Battle of Mohács on August 29, 1526, effectively destroyed the Hungarian monarchy and paved the way for Habsburg and Turkish domination in Hungary.

With the expansion of his authority along the North African coast and the Adriatic shore, it seemed for a time as if the Mediterranean, like the Black Sea and the Aegean, might become an Ottoman lake.

Though it observed the forms of an Islamic legal code, Turkish rule was an unlimited despotism, suffering from none of the financial and constitutional weaknesses of Western states. With its disciplined standing army and its tributary populations, the Ottoman Empire feared no internal threat except during the periods of disputed succession, which continued to occur despite a law empowering the reigning sultan to put to death collateral heirs. It was not unusual for the sultan to take control of frontier provinces, such as Moldavia and Walachia. In Transylvania the voivode John Zápolya gladly accepted Süleyman as his master in return for support against Ferdinand of Austria.

Despite the expeditions of Charles V against Algiers and Tunis, and the inspired resistance of Venice and Genoa in the war of 1537–40, the Ottomans retained control of the Mediterranean until several years after the death of Süleyman. The Knights of St. John were driven from Rhodes and Tripoli and barely succeeded in retaining Malta. Even after Spain, the papacy, Venice, and Genoa had crushed the Turkish armament in 1571 in the Battle of Lepanto, the Ottomans took Cyprus and recovered Tunis from the garrison installed by the allied commander, Don John of Austria. North Africa remained an outpost of Islam, and its corsairs continued to harry Christian shipping, but the Ottoman Empire did not again threaten Europe by land and sea until late in the 17th century.

EASTERN EUROPE

Poland, Lithuania, Bohemia, and Hungary were all loosely associated at the close of the 15th century under rulers of the Jagiellon dynasty. In 1569, three years before the death of the last Jagiellon king of Lithuania-Poland, these two countries merged their separate institutions by the Union of Lublin. Thereafter the Polish nobility and the Roman Catholic faith dominated the Orthodox lands of Lithuania and held the frontiers against Muscovy, the Cossacks, and the Tatars. The Habsburgs regained Bohemia and the vestiges of independent Hungary as a result of dynastic marriages planned by the emperor Maximilian I. When Louis II of Hungary died fighting the Ottomans at Mohács in 1526, Archduke Ferdinand of Austria obtained both crowns and endeavored to affirm the hereditary authority of his dynasty against aristocratic insistence on the principle of election. In 1619, Habsburg claims in Bohemia became the ostensible cause of the Thirty Years' War, when the Diet of Prague momentarily succeeded in deposing Ferdinand II.

In the 16th century, while western Europe was consolidating around monarchs, eastern Europe's aristocracy remained a powerful force. West of the Carpathians and in the lands drained by the Vistula and the Dniester, the landowning class achieved a political independence that weakened the power of monarchy. The towns entered a period of decline, and the propertied class, though divided by rivalry between the magnates and the lesser gentry, everywhere reduced their peasantry to servitude. In Poland and Bohemia the peasants were reduced to serfdom in 1493 and 1497, respectively, and in free Hungary the last peasant rights were suppressed after the rising of 1514. Despite the anarchic quality of Polish politics, the aristocracy maintained and even extended the boundaries of the state. In 1525 they compelled the submission of the secularized Teutonic Order in East Prussia, resisted the pressure of Muscovy, and pressed to the southeast, where communications with the Black Sea had been closed by the Ottomans and their tributaries.

Farther to the east the grand principality of Moscow emerged as a new and powerful despotism. Muscovy, and not Poland, became the heir to Kiev during the reign of Ivan III the Great in the second half of the 15th century. By his marriage with the Byzantine princess Sofia (Zoë) Palaeologus, Ivan also laid claim to the traditions of Constantinople. His capture of Novgorod and repudiation of Tatar overlordship began a movement of Muscovite expansion, which was continued by the seizure of Smolensk by his son Vasily (Basil) III and by the campaigns of his grandson Ivan IV the Terrible (1533–84). The latter destroyed the khanates of Kazan and Astrakhan and reached the Baltic by his conquest of Livonia from Poland and the Knights of the Sword. He was the first to use the title of tsar, and his arbitrary exercise of power was more ruthless and less predictable than that of the Ottoman sultan.

After his death Muscovy was engulfed in the Time of Troubles, when Polish, Swedish, and Cossack armies devastated the land. The accession of the Romanov dynasty in 1613 signaled a period of gradual recovery. Except for occasional embassies, the importation of a few Western artisans, and the reception of Tudor trading missions, Muscovy remained isolated from the West, the Renaissance, and the Reformation.

CHAPTER THREE

THE REFORMATION

In a sense, the Reformation was a protest against the secular values of the Renaissance that had corrupted the Roman Catholic church. The three Renaissance popes, Alexander VI, Julius II, and Leo X, were despots obsessed with materialism and intellectual hedonism. Among those precursors of the reformers who were conscious of the betrayal of Christian ideals were figures so diverse as the Ferraran monk Savonarola, the Spanish statesman Cardinal Jiménez, and the humanist scholar Erasmus. The reform movement at first demanded change from within and ultimately chose the path of separation. In 1517 the Augustinian monk Martin Luther was the first to protest against Pope Leo X, who excommunicated him. In the past, as in the controversies between pope and emperor, such challenges had resulted in mere temporary disunity. In the age of nation-states, though, the dispute had political implications and eventually undermined clerical authority.

THE REFORMATION BEGINS

Luther's eloquent writings evoked a wave of enthusiasm throughout Germany. The reformer was by instinct a social conservative and supported existing secular authority against the upthrust of the lower orders. Although the Diet of Worms accepted the excommunication in 1521, Luther found protection among the princes. In 1529 the rulers of electoral Saxony, Brandenburg, Hessen, Lüneberg, and Anhalt signed the "protest" against an attempt to enforce obedience. By this time, Charles V had resolved to suppress Protestantism and to abandon conciliation. In 1527 his mutinous troops had sacked Rome, which proved a turning point both for the emperor and the humanist movement that he had patronized. The humanist scholars were dispersed, and the initiative for reform then lay in the hands of the more violent and uncompromising party. The empire that Charles V ruled in name was now divided into hostile camps. The Catholic princes of Germany had discussed measures for joint action at Regensburg in 1524; in 1530 the Protestants formed a defensive league at Schmalkalden. Reconciliation was attempted in 1541 and 1548, but the German rift could no longer be healed.

Lutheranism laid its emphasis doctrinally on justification by faith and politically on the God-given powers of the secular ruler. Other Protestants reached different conclusions and diverged widely from one another in their interpretation of the sacraments. In Geneva, Calvinism enforced a stern moral code and proclaimed the separation of church and state, but in practice its organization tended to produce a type of theocracy. Huldrych Zwingli and Heinrich Bullinger

Martin Luther wrote the Ninety-five Theses, a document that came to be considered the catalyst of the Protestant Reformation.

in Zürich taught a theology not unlike Calvin's but preferred to see government in terms of the godly magistrate. On the left wing of these movements were the Anabaptists, whose pacifism and mystic detachment were paradoxically associated with violent upheavals.

Lutheranism established itself in northern Germany and Scandinavia and for a time exercised a wide influence both in eastern Europe and in the west. Where it was not officially adopted by the ruling prince, however, the more militant Calvinist faith tended to take its place. Calvinism spread northward from the upper Rhine and established itself firmly in Scotland and in southern and western France. Friction between Rome and nationalist tendencies within the Catholic church facilitated the spread of Protestantism. In France the Gallican church was traditionally nationalist and antipapal in outlook, while in England the Reformation in its early stages took the form of the preservation of Catholic doctrine and the denial of papal jurisdiction. After periods of Calvinist and then of Roman Catholic reaction, the Church of England achieved a measure of stability with the Elizabethan religious settlement.

THE COUNTER-REFORMATION

The Roman Catholic church responded to the Protestant challenge by purging itself of the abuses and ambiguities that had opened the way to revolt. Thus prepared, the Counter-Reformation embarked upon recovery of the schismatic branches of Western Christianity. Foremost in this crusade were the Jesuits, established as a well-educated and disciplined arm of the papacy by Ignatius Loyola. Their work

Spanish theologian Ignatius of Loyola was one of the most influential figures in the Catholic Reformation of the 16th century and the founder, in 1534, of the Society of Jesus (Jesuits).

was made easier by the Council of Trent, which was held in three parts from 1545 to 1563. The council condemned such abuses as pluralism, affirmed the traditional practice in questions of clerical marriage and the use of the Bible, and clarified doctrine on issues such as the nature of the Eucharist, divine grace, and justification by faith.

The church thus made it clear that it was not prepared to compromise. With the aid of the Inquisition and the material resources of the Habsburgs, it set out to reestablish its universal authority. This could not have been achieved without popes of sincere conviction and initiative who skillfully employed diplomacy, persuasion, and force against heresy. In Italy, Spain, Bavaria, Austria, Bohemia, Poland, and the southern Netherlands (the future Belgium), Protestant influence was destroyed.

DIPLOMACY IN THE AGE OF REFORMATION

The Reformation changed some of the traditional alliances in Europe. For example, Castile and England had been friendly, but that came to an end when the Tudor dynasty embraced Protestantism after 1532. The "auld alliance" between Scotland and France was likewise wrecked by the progress of the Reformation in Scotland after 1560. Moreover, in many countries, religious minorities began to flee to places that embraced their beliefs: for example, the English Catholics to Spain and the French, German, and Dutch Calvinists to England.

These developments created a situation of chronic political instability. On the one hand, the leaders of countries which themselves avoided religious fragmentation (such as

Spain) were often unsure whether to frame their foreign policy according to confessional or political advantage. On the other hand, the foreign policy of religiously divided states, such as France, England, and the Dutch Republic, oscillated often and markedly because there was no consensus among the political elite concerning the correct principles upon which foreign policy should be based.

The complexity of the diplomatic scene called for unusual skills among the rulers of post-Reformation Europe. Seldom has the importance of personality in shaping events been so great. Nevertheless, behind the complicated interplay of individuals and events, two constants may be detected. First, statesmen and churchmen alike consistently identified politics and religion as two sides of the same coin. Supporters of the Bohemian rebellion of 1618, for example, frequently stated that "religion and liberty stand or fall together": that is, a failure to defend and maintain religious liberty would necessarily lead to the loss of political freedom. The position of Emperor Ferdinand II (1619–37) was exactly the same. "God's blessing cannot be received," he informed his subjects, "by a land in which prince and vassals do not both fervently uphold the one true Catholic faith."

These two views, precisely because they were identical, were totally incompatible. That their inevitable collision should have so often produced prolonged wars, however, was due to the second "constant": the desire of political leaders everywhere, even on the periphery of Europe, to secure a balance of power on the continent favourable to their interests. When any struggle became deadlocked, the local rulers looked for foreign support and, more surprisingly, their neighbours were normally ready and eager to provide it. Queen Elizabeth I of England (1558–1603) offered substantial support after 1585 to the Dutch rebels against Philip II and after 1589 to the Protestant Henry IV of France against his more powerful Catholic subjects. Philip II of Spain (1556–98), for his part, sent troops and treasure to the French Catholics, while his son Philip III (1598–1621) did the same for the German Catholics.

This willingness to assist arose because every court in Europe believed in a sort of domino theory, which argued that, if one side won a local war, the rest of Europe would inevitably be affected. The Spanish version of the theory was expressed in a letter from Archduchess Isabella, regent of the Spanish Netherlands, to her master Philip IV in 1623: "It would not be in the interests of Your Majesty to allow the Emperor or the Catholic cause to go down, because of the harm it would do to the possessions of Your Majesty in the Netherlands and Italy." Thus, the religious tensions released by the Reformation eventually pitted two incompatible ideologies against each other. This in turn initiated civil wars that lasted 30 years (in the case of France and Germany) and even 80 years (in the Netherlands), largely because all the courts of Europe saw that the outcome of each confrontation would affect the balance of power for a decade, a generation, perhaps forever.

THE WARS OF RELIGION

Germany, France, and the Netherlands each achieved a settlement of the religious problem by means of war. In Germany, the territorial formula of *cuius regio, eius religio* applied— that is, in each petty state the population had to conform to the religion of the ruler. In France, the Edict of Nantes in 1598 embraced the provisions of previous treaties and accorded the Protestant Huguenots toleration within the state, together with the political and military means of defending the privileges that they had exacted. The southern Netherlands remained Catholic and Spanish, but the Dutch provinces formed an independent Protestant federation in which republican and dynastic influences were nicely balanced. Nowhere was toleration accepted as a positive moral principle, and seldom was it granted except through political necessity.

There were occasions when the Wars of Religion assumed the guise of a supranational conflict between Reformation and Counter-Reformation. Spanish, Savoyard, and papal troops supported the Catholic cause in France against Huguenots aided by Protestant princes in England and Germany. In the Low Countries, English, French, and German armies intervened. At sea Dutch, Huguenot, and English corsairs fought the Battle of the Atlantic against the Spanish champion of the Counter-Reformation. In 1588 the destruction of the Spanish Armada against England was intimately connected with the progress of the struggles in France and the Netherlands.

Behind this ideological grouping of the powers, national, dynastic, and mercenary interests generally

**PREDOMINAN
RELIGIONS IN EUI
mid-16th centu**

Dominant religion

Roman Cath

Lutheran

Calvinist

Church of Er

Eastern Orth

Muslim

Mixed Roma
Catholic, Lut
and Calvinis

Minority religion

Calvinist

Muslim

NORWAY

SCOTLAND

SWEDEN

RUSSIA

IRELAND

NORTH
SEA

DENMARK

BALTIC SEA

ENGLAND

ATLANTIC
OCEAN

LITHUANIA

NETHERLANDS

POLAND

HOLY
ROMAN
EMPIRE

FRANCE   SWITZERLAND

HUNGARY

GAL

OTTOMAN
EMPIRE

SPAIN

PAPAL
STATES

Adriatic Sea

BLACK
SEA

NAPLES

Mediterranean Sea

250   500 mi

50   500 km

Encyclopædia Britannica, Inc.

By the middle of the 16th century, many people who had been Roman Catholic had converted to a Protestant faith, including Lutheranism, Calvinism, or Church of England.

prevailed. The Lutheran duke Maurice of Saxony assisted Charles V in the first Schmalkaldic War in 1547 in order to win the Saxon electoral dignity from his Protestant cousin, John Frederick. Meanwhile, the Catholic king Henry II of France supported the Lutheran cause in the second Schmalkaldic War in 1552 to secure French bases in Lorraine. John Casimir of the Palatinate, the Calvinist champion of Protestantism in France and the Low Countries, maintained an understanding with the neighbouring princes of Lorraine, who led the ultra-Catholic Holy League in France. In the French conflicts, Lutheran German princes served against the Huguenots, and mercenary armies on either side often fought against the defenders of their own religion.

On the one hand, deep divisions separated Calvinist from Lutheran; and, on the other hand, political considerations persuaded the moderate Catholic faction, the Politiques, to oppose the Holy League. The national and religious aspects of the foreign policy of Philip II of Spain were not always in accord. Mutual distrust existed between him and his French allies, the family of Guise, because of their ambitions for their niece Mary Stuart. His desire to perpetuate French weakness through civil war led him at one point to negotiate with the Huguenot leader, Henry of Navarre (afterward Henry IV of France). His policy of religious uniformity in the Netherlands alienated the most wealthy and prosperous part of his dominions. Finally, his ambition to make England and France the satellites of Spain weakened his ability to suppress Protestantism in both countries.

The massacre of Vassy, during which several dozen Huguenots (French Protestants) were killed, was the beginning of the Wars of Religion in France.

THE PEACE OF AUGSBURG

The Peace of Augsburg was the first permanent legal basis for the coexistence of Lutheranism and Catholicism in Germany. It was proclaimed on September 25, 1555, by the Diet of the Holy Roman Empire assembled earlier that year at Augsburg. The Peace allowed the state princes to select either Lutheranism or Catholicism as the religion of their domain and permitted the free emigration of residents who dissented. The legislation officially ended conflict between the two groups, though it made no provisions for other Protestant denominations, such as Calvinism.

The Diet opened at Augsburg on February 5, 1555. Although the assembly was proclaimed by Charles V, he did not wish to take part in the inevitable religious compromises and refused to attend the proceedings. Instead, he empowered his brother Ferdinand (the future emperor Ferdinand I) to settle all questions. The Diet determined that no prince in the empire should make war against another on religious grounds and that this peace should remain operative until the churches were peacefully reunited. Only two churches were recognized, the Roman Catholic and the adherents of the Augsburg Confession—i.e., the Lutherans—and only one church was to be recognized in each territory. Although the religion of the prince's choice was thus made obligatory for his subjects, those who adhered to the other church could sell their property and migrate to a territory where that denomination was recognized. The free imperial cities, which had lost their religious homogeneity a few years earlier, were exceptions to the general ruling; Lutheran and Catholic citizens in these cities remained free to exercise their religion as they pleased. The same freedom was furthermore extended to Lutheran knights and to towns and other communities that had for some time been practicing their religion in the lands of ecclesiastical princes of the empire. This last concession provoked vehement Catholic opposition, and Ferdinand circumvented

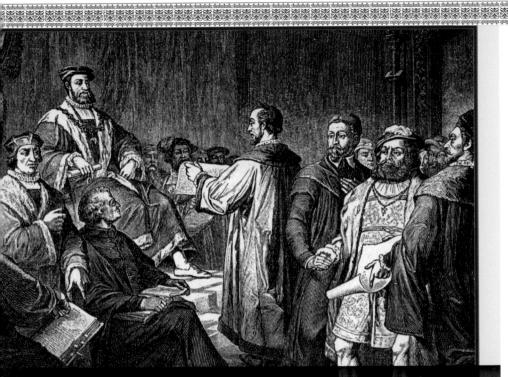

Lutheran princes present their confessions to Ferdinand, who negotiated the Peace of Augsburg.

the difficulty by deciding the matter on his own authority and including the clause in a separate article.

Ecclesiastical lands taken by Lutheran rulers from Catholic prelates who were not immediate vassals of the emperor were to remain with the Lutherans if continuous possession could be proved from the time of the Treaty of Passau (August 2, 1552). However, to ensure the permanence of the remaining ecclesiastical territories, the Catholics gained the condition that in the future any ecclesiastical prince who became Protestant should renounce his office, lands, and revenues. Because the Lutherans would not accept this ecclesiastical reservation and the Catholics would not yield, Ferdinand incorporated the clause on his own authority with a note that agreement had not

(continued on the next page)

(continued from the previous page)

been reached on it. In fact, Lutherans were able to nullify its effect in many cases.

The desire for a lasting settlement was so strong that the compromise peace, which satisfied no one completely and had many loopholes, was accepted. In spite of its shortcomings, the Peace of Augsburg saved the empire from serious internal conflicts for more than 50 years, and Germany thus emerged from the 16th century as a religiously divided country.

In 1562, seven years after the Peace of Augsburg had established a truce in Germany on the basis of territorialism, France became the centre of religious wars that endured, with brief intermissions, for 36 years. The political interests of the aristocracy and the vacillating policy of balance pursued by Henry II's widow, Catherine de Médicis, prolonged these conflicts. After a period of warfare and massacre, Huguenot resistance to the crown was replaced by Catholic opposition to the monarchy's policy of conciliation to Protestants at home and anti-Spanish alliances abroad. The revolt of the Holy League against the prospect of a Protestant king in the person of Henry of Navarre released new forces among the Catholic lower classes, which the aristocratic leadership was unable to control. Eventually Henry won his way to the throne after the extinction of the Valois line, overcame separatist tendencies in the provinces, and secured peace by accepting Catholicism. The policy of the Bourbon dynasty resumed the tradition of Francis I, and under the later guidance of Cardinal Richelieu the potential authority of the monarchy was realized.

In the Netherlands the wise Burgundian policies of Charles V were largely abandoned by Philip II and his lieutenants. Taxation, the Inquisition, and the suppression of privileges for a time provoked the combined resistance of Catholic and Protestant. The house of Orange, represented by William I the Silent and Louis of Nassau, acted as the focus of the revolt. In the undogmatic and flexible personality of William, the rebels found leadership in many ways similar to that of Henry of Navarre. The sack of the city of Antwerp by mutinous Spanish soldiery in 1576 (three years after the dismissal of Philip II's autocratic and capable governor, the duke de Alba) completed the commercial decline of Spain's greatest economic asset. In 1579 Alessandro Farnese, duke di Parma, succeeded in recovering the allegiance of the Catholic provinces, while the Protestant north declared its independence. French and English intervention failed to secure the defeat of Spain, but the dispersal of the Armada and the diversion of Parma's resources to aid the Holy League in France enabled the United Provinces of the Netherlands to survive. A 12-year truce was negotiated in 1609. When the campaign began again, it merged into the general conflict of the Thirty Years' War, which, like the other wars of religion of this period, was fought mainly for confessional security and political gain.

CHAPTER FOUR

THE THIRTY YEARS' WAR BEGINS

he Thirty Years' War originated with dual crises at the continent's centre: one in the Rhineland and the other in Bohemia, both part of the Holy Roman Empire. The Holy Roman Empire of the German Nation was a land of many polities. In the empire there were some 1,000 separate, semiautonomous political units, many of them very small. Others were comparable in size with smaller independent states elsewhere, such as Scotland or the Dutch Republic. The largest section was the lands of the Austrian Habsburgs, covering the elective kingdoms of Bohemia and Hungary, as well as Austria, the Tyrol, and Alsace, with about 8,000,000 inhabitants. Next came electoral Saxony, Brandenburg, and Bavaria, with more than 1,000,000 subjects each; then the Palatinate, Hesse, Trier, and Württemberg, with about 500,000 each.

These were large polities, indeed, but they were weakened by three factors. First, they did not accept primogeniture: Hesse had been divided into four portions at the death of Landgrave Philip the Magnanimous, Luther's patron, in 1567; the lands of the Austrian Habsburgs were partitioned in 1564 and again in 1576. Second, many of the states were geographically fragmented: thus, the Palatinate was divided into an Upper County, adjoining the borders of both Bohemia and Bavaria, and a Lower County, on the middle Rhine. These factors had, in the course of time, created in Germany a balance of power between the states. The territorial strength of the Habsburgs may have brought them a monopoly of the imperial title from 1438 onward, but they could do no more: the other princes, when threatened, were able to form alliances whose military strength was equal to that of the emperor himself.

However, the third weakness—the religious upheaval of the 16th century—changed all that: princes who had formerly stood together were now divided by religion. Swabia, for example, more or less equal in area to modern Switzerland, included 68 secular and 40 spiritual princes and also 32 imperial free cities. By 1618 more than half of these rulers and almost exactly half of the population were Catholic; the rest were Protestant. Neither bloc was prepared to let the other mobilize an army. Similar paralysis was to be found in most other regions: the Reformation and Counter-Reformation had separated Germany into hostile but evenly balanced confessional camps.

THE CRISIS IN GERMANY

The Religious Peace of Augsburg in 1555 had put an end to 30 years of sporadic confessional warfare in Germany between

REKELINCHVSEN

This 17th-century copperplate depicts the War of Cologne (1583–88), a religiously motivated conflict that was a precursor to the Thirty Years' War (1618–48).

Catholics and Lutherans by creating a layered structure of legal securities for the people of the empire. The ecclesiastical reservation, where bishops and abbots who wished to become Lutherans were obliged to resign first, gave rise to a war in 1583–88 when the archbishop of Cologne declared

himself a Protestant but refused to resign. In the end a coalition of Catholic princes, led by the duke of Bavaria, forced him out.

This "War of Cologne" was a turning point in the religious history of Germany. Until then, the Catholics had been on the defensive, losing ground steadily to the Protestants. Even the decrees of the Council of Trent, which animated Catholics elsewhere, failed to strengthen the position of the Roman church in Germany. After the successful struggle to retain Cologne, however, Catholic princes began to enforce the *cuius regio, eius religio* ("whose realm, his religion") principle. In Bavaria, as well as in Würzburg, Bamberg, and other ecclesiastical states, Protestants were given the choice of either conversion or exile. Most of those affected were adherents of the Lutheran church, already weakened by defections to Calvinism, a new creed that had scarcely a German adherent at the time of the Religious Peace of Augsburg. The rulers of the Palatinate (1560), Nassau (1578), Hesse-Kassel (1603), and Brandenburg (1613) all abandoned Lutheranism for the new confession, as did many lesser rulers and several towns. Small wonder that the Lutherans came to detest the Calvinists even more than they loathed the Catholics.

These religious divisions created a complex pattern in Germany. By the first decade of the 17th century, the Catholics were firmly entrenched south of the Danube and the Lutherans northeast of the Elbe; but the areas in between

This engraving depicts a procession of the Catholic League through Paris.

THE CATHOLIC LEAGUE

The Catholic League (in German, Katholische Liga) was a military alliance (1609–35) of the Catholic powers of Germany led by Maximilian I, duke of Bavaria, and designed to stem the growth of Protestantism in Germany. In alliance with the Habsburg emperors, the League's forces, led by Johann Tserclaes, Graf von Tilly, played a key role in the Thirty Years' War.

Plans for a league had long been discussed, but the formation of the Protestant Union in 1608 caused the Catholics to unite under Maximilian. The original League members on July 10, 1609, included Bavaria and the prince-bishops of Bavaria, Franconia, and Swabia. The Rhenish ecclesiastical electors of Mainz, Trier, and Cologne joined on July 30 of that year. Maximilian reorganized the League in 1617, excluding the Rhenish members and making the League an exclusively southern German confederation.

The Bohemian revolt of 1618 caused alarm among the German Catholics, and the League resumed its expanded form in May 1619. When the Protestant elector Frederick V of the Palatinate accepted the Bohemian crown later that year, the Holy Roman Emperor Ferdinand II looked to the League for military support. Through negotiations in 1620, Maximilian undermined the Protestant Union's support of Frederick. In November 1620, the League's forces under Tilly crushed Frederick at the Battle of White Mountain near Prague. Tilly's troops then

(continued on the next page)

(continued from the previous page)

ravaged the Palatinate and other Protestant lands to the north; won several battles over King Christian IV of Denmark, who had come to the Protestants' defense; and helped carry out Catholic restitutions in conquered Protestant territories. The importance of the League began to decline after 1626, when the Emperor found his own general in Albrecht von Wallenstein. Tilly's defeat by Gustav II Adolf of Sweden at Breitenfeld in 1631, followed by his death the following year, accelerated the League's decline. It was abolished in 1635 by the Peace of Prague, which forbade military confederations in the Empire.

were a patchwork quilt of Calvinist, Lutheran, and Catholic, and in some places one could find all three. One such was Donauwörth, an independent city just across the Danube from Bavaria, obliged (by the Peace of Augsburg) to tolerate both Catholics and Protestants. But for years the Catholic minority had not been permitted full rights of public worship. When in 1606 the priests tried to hold a procession through the streets, they were beaten and their relics and banners were desecrated. Shortly afterward, an Italian Capuchin, Fray Lorenzo da Brindisi, later canonized, arrived in the city and was himself mobbed by a Lutheran crowd chanting "Capuchin, Capuchin, scum, scum." He heard from the local clergy of their plight and promised to find redress. Within a year, Fray Lorenzo had secured promises of aid from Duke Maximilian of Bavaria and Emperor Rudolf II. When the Lutheran magistrates of Donauwörth flatly refused to permit their Catholic subjects freedom of worship, the Bavarians marched into the city and restored Catholic worship by force (December 1607). Maximilian's men also banned Protestant worship and set up an occupation government that eventually transferred the city to direct Bavarian rule.

These dramatic events thoroughly alarmed Protestants elsewhere in Germany. Was this, they wondered, the first step in a new Catholic offensive against heresy? Elector Frederick IV of the Palatinate took the lead. On May 14, 1608, he formed the Evangelical, or Protestant, Union, an association to last for 10 years, for self-defense. At first, membership remained restricted to Germany, although the elector's leading adviser, Christian of Anhalt, wished to extend it, but before long a new crisis rocked the empire and turned the German union into a Protestant International.

The new crisis began with the death of John William, the childless duke of Cleves-Jülich, in March 1609. His duchies, occupying a strategic position in the Lower Rhineland, had both Protestant and Catholic subjects, but both of the main claimants to the inheritance were Protestants; under the *cuius regio* principle, their succession would lead to the expulsion of the Catholics. The emperor therefore refused to recognize the Protestant princes' claim. Since both were members of the Union, they solicited, and received, promises of military aid from their colleagues; they also received, via Christian of Anhalt, similar promises from the kings of France and England. This sudden growth in Protestant strength caused the German Catholics to take countermeasures: a Catholic League was formed between Duke Maximilian of Bavaria and his neighbours on July 10, 1609, soon to be joined by the ecclesiastical rulers of the Rhineland and receiving support

Rudolf II was Holy Roman emperor from 1576 to 1612. His ill health and unpopularity prevented him from restraining the religious dissensions that eventually led to the Thirty Years' War.

from Spain and the Papacy. Again, reinforcement for one side provoked counter-measures. The Union leaders signed a defensive treaty with England in 1612 (cemented by the marriage of the Union's director, the young Frederick V of the Palatine, to the king of England's daughter) and with the Dutch Republic in 1613.

All these alliances were motivated by fear of religious extinction. The Union members were con-vinced of the existence of a Catholic conspiracy aimed at rooting out all traces of Protestantism from the empire. This view was shared by the Union's foreign supporters. At the time of the Cleves-Jülich succession crisis, Sir Ralph Winwood, an English diplomat at the heart of affairs, wrote to his masters that, although "the issue of this whole business, if slightly considered, may seem trivial and ordinary," in reality its outcome would "uphold or cast down the greatness of the house of Austria and the church of Rome in these quarters." Such fears were prob-ably unjustified at this time. In 1609 the unity of purpose between pope and emperor was in fact far from perfect, and the last thing Maximilian of Bavaria wished to see was

Habsburg participation in the League: rather than suffer it, in 1614 he formed a separate association of his own and in 1616 he resigned from the League altogether. This reduction in the Catholic threat was enough to produce reciprocal moves among the Protestants. Although there was renewed fighting in 1614 over Cleves-Jülich, the members of the Protestant Union had abandoned their militant stance by 1618, when the treaty of alliance came up for renewal. They declared that they would no longer become involved in the territorial wrangles of individual members, and they resolved to prolong their association for only three years more.

THE CRISIS IN THE HABSBURG LANDS

While the Cleves-Jülich crisis held the attention of western Europe in 1609, the eyes of observers farther east were on Prague, the capital of Bohemia. That elective kingdom (which also included Silesia, Lusatia, and Moravia), together with Hungary, had come to the Habsburg family in 1526. At first they were ruled jointly with Austria by Ferdinand I (brother of Emperor Charles V), but after his death in 1564 the inheritance was divided into three portions: Alsace and Tyrol (known as "Further Austria") went to one of his younger sons; Styria, Carinthia, and Carniola (known as "Inner Austria") went to a second; only the remainder was left for his successor as emperor, Maximilian II.

By 1609 fragmentation had advanced even further: Maximilian's eldest son, Rudolf II (emperor, 1576–1611), ruled only Bohemia; all the rest of his father's territories had been acquired, the previous year, by a younger son, Matthias. The new ruler had come to power not through strength or talent, however, but by the exploitation of the religious divisions of his subjects. During the 1570s the Protestants of Austria, Bohemia, and Hungary had used their strength of numbers and control of local representative assemblies to force the Habsburgs to grant freedom of worship to their Protestant subjects. This was clearly against the *cuius regio* principle, and everyone knew it. In 1599 the ruler of Inner Austria, Archduke Ferdinand, began a campaign of forcible re-Catholicization among his subjects, which proved entirely successful. But, when Rudolf II launched the same policy in Hungary shortly afterward, there was a revolt, and the rebels offered the Hungarian crown to Matthias in return for guarantees of toleration. The Bohemians decided to exploit Rudolf's temporary embarrassment by pressing him to grant similarly far-reaching concessions to the non-Catholic majority of that kingdom. The "Letter of Majesty" (Majestätsbrief) signed by Rudolf on July 9, 1609, granted full toleration to Protestants and created a standing committee of the Estates, known as "the Defensors," to ensure that the settlement would be respected.

Rudolf II—a recluse who hid in a world of fantasy and alchemy in his Hradčany palace above Prague, a manic depressive who tried to take his own life on at least one occasion—proved to be incapable of keeping to the same policy for long. In 1611 he tried to revoke the Letter of Majesty and to depose the Defensors by sending a small Habsburg army into Prague, but a force of superior strength was mobilized against the invaders and the Estates resolved to depose Rudolf and offer their crown to Matthias. The emperor, broken in mind and body, died in January 1612. All his territories were then ruled by his brother, who also succeeded him as

Holy Roman emperor later in the year. The alliance with the Protestant Estates that brought about Matthias's elevation, however, did not long continue once he was in power. The new ruler sought to undo the concessions he had made, and he looked for support to his closest Habsburg relatives: his brother Albert, ruler of the Spanish Netherlands; his cousin Ferdinand, ruler of Inner Austria; and his nephew Philip III, king of Spain. All three, however, turned him down.

Albert had in 1609 succeeded in bringing the war between Spain and the Dutch Republic to a temporary close with the Twelve Years' Truce. The last thing he wanted was to involve his ravaged country in supplying men and money to Vienna, perhaps provoking countermeasures from Protestants nearer home. Archduke Ferdinand, although willing to aid Matthias to uphold his authority (not least because he regarded himself as heir presumptive to the childless Matthias), was prevented from doing so by the outbreak of war between his Croatian subjects and the neighbouring republic of Venice (the Uskok War, 1615–18). Philip of Spain was also involved in war: in 1613–15 and 1616–17, Spanish forces in Lombardy fought the troops of the duke of Savoy over the succession to the childless duke of Mantua. Spain could therefore aid neither Matthias nor Ferdinand.

In 1617, however, papal diplomats secured a temporary settlement of the Mantuan question, and Spanish troops hastened to the aid of Ferdinand. Before long, Venice made overtures for peace, and the archduke was able to leave his capital at Graz in order to join Matthias. The emperor, old and infirm, was anxious to establish Ferdinand as his heir, and, in the autumn of 1617, the Estates of both Bohemia and Hungary were persuaded to recognize the archduke unconditionally

In the incident known as the defenestration of Prague, two Catholic regents and their secretary were thrown from the windows of the council room of Hradčany (Prague Castle).

as king-designate. On the strength of this, Ferdinand proceeded over the winter of 1617–18 to halt the concessions being made to Protestants. He created a council of regency for Bohemia that was overwhelmingly Catholic, and it soon began to censor works printed in Prague and to prevent

non-Catholics from holding government office. More inflammatory still, the regents ordered Protestant worship to stop in towns on church lands (which they claimed were not included in the Letter of Majesty).

The Defensors created by the Letter of Majesty expressed strong objection to these measures and summoned the Estates of the realm to meet in May 1618. When the regents declared the meeting illegal, the Estates invaded the council chamber and threw two Catholic regents, together with their secretary, from the window. Next, a provisional government (known as the Directors) was created and a small army was raised.

Apart from the famous "defenestration," the events in Prague in May 1618 were, superficially, little different from those in 1609 and 1611. Yet no 30-year struggle arose from those earlier crises. The crucial difference lay in the involvement of foreign powers: in 1609 and 1611 the Habsburgs, represented by Rudolf and Matthias, had given in to their subjects' demands; in 1618, led by Ferdinand, they did not. At first his defiant stance achieved nothing, for the army of the rebels expelled loyal troops from almost every part of the kingdom while their diplomats secured declarations of support from

Silesia, Lusatia, and Upper Austria almost at once and from Moravia and Lower Austria shortly afterward. In May 1619 the rebel army even laid siege to Ferdinand in Vienna. Within weeks, however, they were forced to withdraw because a major Spanish army, partly financed by the pope, invaded Bohemia.

The appearance of Spanish troops and papal gold in eastern Europe immediately reawakened the fears of the Protestant rulers of the empire. To the government of Philip III, led by the former ambassador in Vienna, Don Balthasar de Zúñiga, the choice had seemed clear: "Your Majesty should consider," wrote one minister, "which will be of the greater service to you: the loss of these provinces [to the house of Habsburg], or the dispatch of an army of 15 to 20 thousand men to settle the matter." Seen in these terms, Spain could scarcely avoid military intervention in favour of Ferdinand; but to Protestant observers the logic of Spanish intervention seemed aggressive rather than defensive. Dudley Carleton, the English ambassador to the Dutch Republic, observed that the new emperor "flatters himself with prophesies of extirpating the Reformed religion and restoring the Roman church to the ancient greatness" and accurately predicted that, if the Protestant cause were to be "neglected and by consequence suppressed, the Protestant princes adjoining [Bohemia] are like to bear the burden of a victorious army."

This same argument carried weight with the director of the Protestant Union, Frederick V of the Palatinate, parts of whose territories adjoined Bohemia. So, when in the summer of 1619 the Bohemians deposed Ferdinand and offered the crown to Frederick, he was favourably disposed. Some of the elector's advisers favoured rejecting this offer, since "acceptance would surely begin a general religious war." But others pointed out that such a war was inevitable anyway when the Twelve Years' Truce between Spain and the Dutch Republic expired in April 1621 and argued that allowing the Bohemian cause to fail would merely ensure that the conflict in the Netherlands would be resolved in Spain's favour later, making a concerted Habsburg attack on the Protestants of the empire both ineluctable and irresistible.

Frederick accepted the Bohemian crown and in so doing rekindled the worst fears of the German Catholics. The Catholic League was re-created, and in December 1619 its leaders authorized the levy of an army of 25,000 men to be used as Maximilian of Bavaria thought fit. At the same time, Philip III and Archduke Albert each promised to send a new army into Germany to assist Ferdinand (who had succeeded the late Matthias as Holy Roman emperor). The crisis was now apparent. The underlying cause for the outbreak of a war that would last 30 years was the pathological fear of a Catholic conspiracy among the Protestants and the equally entrenched suspicion of a Protestant conspiracy among the Catholics.

CHAPTER FIVE

MILITARY CAMPAIGNS OF THE THIRTY YEARS' WAR

Frederick V entered Prague and was crowned king by the rebel Estates in October 1619, but already the Catholic net was closing around him. The axis linking Vienna with Munich, Brussels, and Madrid enjoyed widespread support: subsidies came from Rome and Genoa, while Tuscany and Poland sent troops. Equally serious, states favourable to Frederick's cause were persuaded to remain neutral: Spanish diplomacy kept England out of the war, while French efforts persuaded the Protestant Union to remain aloof from the Bohemian adventure of their leader. The Dutch Republic also did nothing, so that in the summer of 1620 a Spanish army was able to cross from the Netherlands and occupy the Rhine Palatinate. Meanwhile, the armies of the emperor and League, reinforced with Spanish and Italian contingents, invaded the rebel heartland. On November 8, in the first significant battle of the war, at the White Mountain outside Prague, Frederick's forces were routed. The unfortunate prince fled northward, abandoning his subjects to the mercy of the victorious Ferdinand.

This was total victory, and it might have remained the last word but for events in the Low Countries. Once the Twelve Years' Truce expired in April 1621, the Dutch, fearing a concerted attack by both Spanish and Austrian Habsburgs, decided to provide an asylum for the defeated Frederick and to supply diplomatic and, eventually, military assistance to his cause. In 1622 and again in 1623, armies were raised for Frederick with Dutch money, but they were defeated. Worse, the shattered armies retreated toward the Netherlands, drawing the Catholic forces behind them. It began to seem that a joint Habsburg invasion of the republic was inevitable after all.

THE TRIUMPH OF THE CATHOLICS, 1619–29

Frederick's political position, however, weakened considerably in the course of 1623. Although his armies won impressive victories in the field, they were only able to do so thanks to massive financial and military support from the Catholic League, controlled by Maximilian of Bavaria. Ferdinand II, thanks to the Spanish and papal subsidies, maintained some 15,000 men himself, but the League provided him with perhaps 50,000. Thus, Maximilian's armies had, in effect, won Ferdinand's victories and, now that all common enemies had been defeated, Maximilian requested his reward: the lands and electoral title of the outlawed Frederick of the Palatinate. Don Balthasar de Zúñiga, chief minister of Ferdinand's other

The Catholic victory in the Battle of White Mountain enabled the house of Habsburg to establish an authoritarian government that survived for three centuries.

major ally, Spain, warned that the consequences of acceding to this demand could be serious. However, in October 1622 he died, and no one else in Madrid—least of all his successor as principal minister, the Count-Duke of Olivares—had practical experience of German affairs. Therefore, in January

1623 the emperor felt able to proceed with the investiture of Maximilian as elector Palatine.

Zúñiga, however, had been right: the electoral transfer provoked an enormous outcry, for it was clearly unconstitutional. The Golden Bull of 1356, which was universally regarded in Germany as the fundamental and immutable law of the empire, ordained that the electorate should remain in the Palatine house in perpetuity. The transfer of 1623 thus undermined a cornerstone of the Constitution, which many regarded as their only true safeguard against absolute rule. Inside Germany, a pamphlet war against Maximilian and Ferdinand began; outside, sympathy for Frederick at last created that international body of support for his cause that had previously been so conspicuously lacking. The Dutch and the Palatine exiles found little difficulty in engineering an alliance involving France, England, Savoy, Sweden, and Denmark that was dedicated to the restoration of Frederick to his forfeited lands and titles (the Hague Alliance, December 9, 1624). Its leader was Christian IV of Denmark (1588–1648), one of the richest rulers in Christendom, who saw a chance to extend his influence in northern Germany under cover of defending "the Protestant cause." He invaded the empire in June 1625.

The Protestants' diplomatic campaign had not gone unnoticed, however. Maximilian's field commander, Count Tilly, warned that his forces alone would be no match for a coalition army and asked that the emperor send reinforcements. Ferdinand obliged: in the spring of 1625 he authorized Albrecht von Wallenstein, military governor of Prague, to raise an imperial army of 25,000 men and to move it northward to meet the Danish threat. Wallenstein's approach forced Christian to withdraw; when the Danes invaded again the following year, they were routed at the Battle of Lutter (August 26, 1626). The joint armies of Tilly and Wallenstein pursued the defeated forces: first they occupied the lands of North German rulers who had declared support for the invasion, then they conquered the Danish mainland itself. Christian made peace in 1629, promising never again to intervene in the empire. His allies had long since withdrawn from the struggle.

The White Mountain delivered the Bohemian rebels into the emperor's grasp; Lutter delivered the rebels' German supporters. After the victories, Ferdinand initiated important new policies that aimed at exalting the Catholic religion and his own authority. In the Habsburg provinces there was widespread confiscation of land—perhaps two-thirds of the kingdom of Bohemia changed hands during the 1620s—and a new class of loyal landowners—like Wallenstein—was established. At the same time, the power of the Estates was curtailed and freedom of worship for Protestants was restricted (in some territories) or abolished (in most of the rest). Even a rebellion in Upper Austria in 1626, provoked principally by the persecution of Protestants, failed to change Ferdinand's mind. Indeed, fortified by his success in the Habsburg lands, he decided to implement new policies in the empire.

First, disloyal rulers were replaced (the Palatinate went to Maximilian, Mecklenburg to Wallenstein, and so on). Next, serious steps were taken to reclaim church lands that had fallen into Protestant hands. At first this was done on a piecemeal basis, but on March 28, 1629, an Edict of Restitution was issued that declared unilaterally that all church lands secularized since 1552 must be returned at once, that Calvinism was an illegal creed in the empire, and that ecclesiastical princes had the same right as secular ones to insist that their subjects should be of the same religion as their ruler. The last

Albrecht von Wallenstein was commanding general of Ferdinand II's armies, but his alienation from the emperor and his political-military conspiracies led to his assassination.

clause, at least, was clearly contrary to the terms of the Peace of Augsburg, which Protestants regarded as a central pillar of the Constitution. There was, however, no opportunity for argument, for the imperial edict was enforced immediately, brutally, by the armies of Wallenstein and Tilly, which now numbered some 200,000 men. The people of the empire seemed threatened with an arbitrary rule against which they had no defense. It was this fear, skillfully exploited once again by Protestant propagandists, that ensured that the war in Germany did not end in 1629 with the defeat of Denmark. Ferdinand may have won numerous military victories, but in

Die betrangte Stadt Augspurg.

This political cartoon represents the Edict of Restitution, in which the two large creatures symbolize Catholicism swallowing the city of Augsburg.

doing so he had suffered a serious political defeat. The pens of his enemies proved mightier than the sword.

THE CRISIS OF THE WAR, 1629–35

If Maximilian of Bavaria desired the title of elector as his reward for supporting Ferdinand, Spain (for its part) required imperial support for its war against the Dutch. When repeated requests for a direct invasion by Wallenstein's army remained unanswered (largely due to Bavarian opposition), Spain began to think of creating a Baltic navy, with imperial assistance, which would cleanse the inland sea of Dutch shipping and thus administer a body blow to the republic's economy. But the plan aborted, for the imperial army failed in 1628 to conquer the port of Stralsund, selected as the base for the new fleet. Now, with Denmark defeated, Madrid again pleaded for the loan of an imperial army, and this time the request was granted. In the end, however, the troops did not march to the Netherlands: instead, they went to Italy.

The death of the last native ruler of the strategic states of Mantua and Montferrat in December 1627 created dangers in Italy that the Spaniards were unable to ignore and temptations that they were unable to resist. Hoping to forestall intervention by others, Spanish forces from Lombardy launched an invasion, but the garrisons of Mantua and Montferrat declared for the late duke's relative, the French-born duke of Nevers. Nevers lacked the resources to withstand the forces of Spain alone, and he appealed to France for support. Louis XIII (1610–43) and Cardinal Richelieu (chief minister 1624–42) were, however, engaged in a desperate war against their Calvinist subjects. Only when the rebels had been defeated, early in 1629, was it possible for the king and his chief minister to cross the Mount Cenis Pass and enter Italy. Philip IV of Spain (1621–25) asked the emperor to meet this threat, sending his troops to Italy rather than to the Netherlands. When Louis XIII launched a second invasion in 1630, some 50,000 imperial troops were brought south to oppose them, reducing the war for Mantua to a stalemate but delivering the Dutch Republic from immediate danger and weakening the emperor's hold on Germany.

Gustav II Adolf of Sweden (1611–32) had spent most of the 1620s at war with Poland, seeking to acquire territory on the southern shore of the Baltic. By the Truce of Altmark

(September 26, 1629), with the aid of French and British mediators, Poland made numerous concessions in return for a six-year truce. Gustav lost no time in redeploying his forces: on July 6, 1630, he led a Swedish expeditionary force ashore near Stralsund with the declared intention of saving the "liberties of the empire" and preserving the security of the Baltic.

Despite the defeat of the German Protestants and their allies, Sweden's position was far more favourable than that of Denmark five years earlier. Instead of the two armies that had faced Christian IV, Gustav was opposed by only one, for in the summer of 1630 the emperor's Catholic allies in Germany—led by Maximilian of Bavaria—demanded the dismissal of Wallenstein and the drastic reduction of his expensive army. It was an ultimatum that Ferdinand, with the bulk of his forces tied down in the war of Mantua, could not ignore, even though he thereby lost the services of the one man who might conceivably have retained all the imperial gains of the previous decade and united Germany under a strong monarchy.

The emperor and his German allies, nevertheless, did remain united over the Edict of Restitution: there were to be no concessions in matters of religion and no restoration of forfeited lands. As a result, the German Protestants were driven reluctantly into the arms of Sweden, whose army was increased with the aid of subsidies secured from France and the Dutch. In Septem-

The Battle of Lützen, in which Gustav was killed, was fought by the Swedes to help their north German allies against the forces of the Holy Roman Emperor Ferdinand II.

ber 1631 Gustav at last felt strong enough to challenge the emperor's forces in battle: at Breitenfeld, just outside Leipzig in Saxony, he was totally victorious. The main Catholic field army was destroyed, and the Swedish Protestant host overran most of central Germany and Bohemia in the winter of 1631–32. The next summer they occupied Bavaria.

ATTEMPTS AT PEACE

The Peace of Prague in 1635 ended the conflict between Ferdinand II and the Protestant states of the Holy Roman Empire. This partial settlement of the issues behind the war led many in Germany to look forward to a general peace. Certainly the exhaustion of many areas of the empire was a powerful incentive to end the war. The population of Lutheran Württemberg, for example, which was occupied by the imperialists between 1634 and 1638, fell from 450,000 to 100,000; material damage was estimated at 34 million thalers. Mecklenburg and Pomerania, occupied by the Swedes, had suffered in proportion. Even a city like Dresden, the capital of Saxony, which was neither besieged nor occupied, saw its demographic balance change from 121 baptisms for every 100 burials in the 1620s to 39 baptisms for every 100 burials in the 1630s. Amid such catastrophes an overwhelming sense of war-weariness engulfed Germany.

Attempts were made to convert the Peace of Prague into a general settlement. At a meeting of the electors held at Regensburg in 1636–37, Ferdinand II agreed to pardon any prince who submitted to him and promised to begin talks with the foreign powers to discover their terms for peace. But the emperor's death immediately after the meeting ended this initiative. Efforts by Pope Urban VIII (1623–44) to convene a general conference at Cologne were similarly unavailing. Then, in 1640, the new emperor, Ferdinand III (1637–57), assembled the Imperial Diet for the first time since 1613 in order to solve at least the outstanding German problems of the amnesty question and the restitution of church lands. He met with little success and could not prevent first Brandenburg (1641) and then Brunswick (1642) from making a separate agreement with Sweden. The problem was that none of these attempts at peace were acceptable to France and Sweden, yet no lasting settlement could be made without them.

Although Gustav died in battle at Lützen on Nov. 16, 1632, his forces were again victorious and his chief adviser, Axel Oxenstierna, directed the cause with equal skill. In the east, Sweden managed to engineer a Russian invasion of Poland in the autumn of 1632 that tied down the forces of both powers for almost two years.

Meanwhile, in Germany, Oxenstierna crafted a military alliance that transferred much of the cost of the war onto the shoulders of the German Protestant states (the Heilbronn League, April 23, 1633). Swedish ascendancy, however, was destroyed in 1634 when Russia made peace with Poland (at Polyanov, June 4) and Spain sent a large army across the Alps from Lombardy to join the imperial forces at the Battle of Nördlingen (September 6). This time the Swedes were decisively beaten and were obliged to withdraw their forces in haste from most of southern Germany.

Yet Sweden, under Oxenstierna's skillful direction, fought on. Certainly its motives included a desire to defend the Protestant cause in Germany and to restore deposed princes to their thrones. But more important by far was the fear that, if the German Protestants were finally defeated, the imperialists would turn the Baltic into a Habsburg lake and might perhaps invade Sweden. The Stockholm government therefore desired a settlement that would splinter the empire into a jumble of independent, weak states incapable of threatening the security of Sweden or its hold on the Baltic. Furthermore, to guarantee this fragmentation, Oxenstierna desired the transfer to his country of sovereignty over certain strategic areas of the empire—particularly the duchy of Pomerania on the Baltic coast and the electorate of Mainz on the Rhine.

These, however, were not at all the goals of Sweden's German allies. They aimed rather at the restoration of the prewar situation—in which there had been no place for Sweden—and it soon became clear that they were prepared to make a separate settlement with the emperor in order to achieve it. No sooner was Gustav dead than the elector of Saxony, as "foremost Lutheran prince of the Empire," put out peace feelers toward Vienna. At first John George (1611–56) was adamant about the need to abolish the Edict of Restitution and to secure a full amnesty for all as preconditions for a settlement. However, the imperial victory at Nördlingen made him less demanding. The insistence on an amnesty for Frederick V was dropped, and it was accepted that the edict would be applied in all areas recovered by Catholic forces before November 1627 (roughly speaking, all lands south of the Elbe, but not the Lutheran heartland of Saxony and Brandenburg). The elector might have been required to make even more concessions but for the fact that, over the winter of 1634–35, French troops began to mass along Germany's borders. As the papal nuncio in Vienna observed: "If the French intervene in Germany, the emperor will be forced to conclude peace with Saxony on whatever terms he can." So the Peace of Prague was signed between the emperor and the Saxons on May 30, 1635, and within a year most other German Lutherans also changed their allegiance from Stockholm to Vienna.

THE EUROPEAN WAR IN GERMANY, 1635–45

After the Peace of Prague, the nature of the Thirty Years' War was transformed. Instead of being principally a struggle between the emperor and his own subjects, with some foreign aid, it became a war of the emperor against foreign powers whose German supporters were, at most times, few in number and limited in resources. Sweden, as noted above, had distinct and fairly consistent war aims: to secure some bases in the empire, both as guarantees of influence in the postwar era and as some recompense for coming to the rescue of the Protestants, and to create a system of checks and balances in Germany, which would mean that no single power would ever again become dominant. If those aims could be achieved, Oxenstierna was prepared to quit. As he wrote, "We must let this German business be left to the Germans, who will be the only people to get any good out of it (if there is any), and therefore not spend any more men or money, but rather try by all means to wriggle out of it."

But how could these objectives be best achieved? The Heilbronn League did not long survive the Battle of Nördlingen and the Peace of Prague, and so it became necessary to find an alternative source of support. The only one available was France. Louis XIII and Richelieu, fresh from their triumph in Italy, had been subsidizing Sweden's war effort for some time. In 1635, in the wake of Nördlingen, they signed an offensive and defensive alliance with the Dutch Republic (February 8), with Sweden (April 28), and with Savoy (July 11). They also sent an army into the Alps to occupy the Valtelline, a strategic military link between the possessions of the Spanish and Austrian Habsburgs (March); and they mediated a 20-year truce between Sweden and Poland (September 12). Finally, on May 19, 1635, they declared war on Spain.

The aims of France were very different from those of Sweden and its German allies. France wished to defeat Spain,

The Battle of Wittstock was a badly needed Swedish victory that improved the prospects of the Protestant cause after the overwhelming defeat at Nördlingen in 1634.

its rival for more than a century, and its early campaigns in Germany were intended more to prevent Ferdinand from sending aid to his Spanish cousins than to impose a Bourbon solution on Germany—indeed, France only declared war on Ferdinand in March 1636. Sweden at first therefore avoided a firm commitment to France, leaving the way clear for a separate peace should the military situation improve sufficiently to permit the achievement of its own particular aims.

The war, however, did not go in favour of the allies. French and Swedish forces, operating separately, totally failed to reverse the verdict of Nördlingen: despite the Swedish victory at Wittstock (October 4, 1636) and French gains in Alsace and the middle Rhine (1638), the Habsburgs always seemed able to even up the score. Thus, in 1641 Oxenstierna abandoned his attempt to maintain independence and threw in his lot with France. By the terms of the Treaty of Hamburg (March 15, 1641), the two sides promised not to make a separate peace. Instead, joint negotiations with the emperor and the German princes for the satisfaction of the allies' claims were to begin in the

Westphalian towns of Münster and Osnabrück. And, while the talks proceeded, the war was to continue.

The Treaty of Hamburg had at last created a coalition capable of destroying the power both of Ferdinand III and of Maximilian of Bavaria. On the whole, France attacked Bavaria, and Sweden fought the emperor, but there was considerable interchange of forces and a carefully coordinated strategy. On November 2, 1642, the Habsburgs' army was routed in Saxony at the Second Battle of Breitenfeld, and the emperor was saved from further defeat only by the outbreak of war between Denmark and Sweden (May 1643–August 1645). Yet, even before Denmark's final surrender, the Swedes were back in Bohemia, and at Jankov (March 6, 1645) they totally destroyed another imperial army. The emperor and his family fled to Graz, while the Swedes advanced to the Danube and threatened Vienna. Reinforcements were also sent to assist the French campaign against Bavaria, and on August 3 Maximilian's forces were decisively defeated at Allerheim.

Jankov and Allerheim were two of the truly decisive battles of the war, because they destroyed all possibility of the Catholics' obtaining a favourable peace settlement. In September 1645 the elector of Saxony made a separate peace with Sweden and so—like Brandenburg and Brunswick before him—in effect withdrew from the war. Meanwhile, at the peace conference in session in Westphalia, the imperial delegation began to make major concessions: Oxenstierna noted with satisfaction that, since Jankov, "the enemy begins to talk more politely and pleasantly." He was confident that peace was just around the corner. He was wrong.

CHAPTER SIX

AFTERMATH OF THE THIRTY YEARS' WAR

One hundred and ninety-four European rulers, great and small, were represented at the Congress of Westphalia, and talks went on constantly from the spring of 1643 until the autumn of 1648. The outstanding issues of the war were solved in two phases. The first, which lasted from November 1645 until June 1647, saw the chief imperial negotiator, Maximilian, Count Trauttmannsdorf, settle most issues. The second, which continued from then until the treaty of peace was signed in October 1648, saw France try to sabotage the agreements already made.

RESOLUTION IN GERMANY

The purely German problems were resolved first, partly because they were already near solution. So in 1645 and 1646, with the aid of French and Swedish mediation, the territorial

The Swearing of the Oath of Ratification of the Treaty of Münster, oil on copper by Gerard Terborch, 1648, depicts the settlement of the Peace of Westphalia.

rulers were granted a large degree of sovereignty (*Landesho-heit*), and a general amnesty was issued to all German princes. An eighth electorate was created for the son of Frederick V (so that both he and Maximilian possessed the coveted dignity). The Edict of Restitution was finally abandoned, and Calvinism within the empire was granted official toleration. The last two points were the most bitterly argued and led to the division of the German rulers at the Congress into two blocs: the Corpus Catholicorum and the Corpus Evangelicorum. Neither was monolithic or wholly united, but eventually the Catholics split into those who were prepared to make religious concessions in order to have peace and those who were not.

A coalition of Protestants and pragmatic Catholics then succeeded in securing the acceptance of a formula that recognized as Protestant all church lands in secular hands by January 1, 1624 (that is, before the gains made by Wallenstein and Tilly) and granted freedom of worship to religious minorities where these had existed by the same date. The Augsburg settlement of 1555 was thus entirely overthrown, and it was agreed that any change to the new formula must be achieved only through the "amicable composition" of the Catholic and Protestant blocs, not by a simple majority. All parties finally accepted the amicable composition principle early in 1648, thus solving the last German problem.

RESOLUTION IN THE NETHERLANDS, SWEDEN, AND FRANCE

However, because so many foreign powers were involved in the war, the resolution of the German problems did not lead to immediate peace. Apart from France and Sweden, representatives from the Dutch Republic, Spain, and many other non-German participants in the war were present, each of them eager to secure the best settlement they could.

The war in the Netherlands was the first to be ended: on January 30, 1648, Philip IV of Spain signed a peace that recognized the Dutch Republic as independent and agreed to liberalize trade between the Netherlands and the Iberian world. The French government, led since Richelieu's death (December 4, 1642) by Jules Cardinal Mazarin (Giulio Mazzarino), was bitterly opposed to this settlement, since it left Spain free to deploy all its forces in the Low Countries against France. As a consequence, France devoted all

THE FRONDE

The Fronde (in French, La Fronde) was a series of civil wars in France between 1648 and 1653, during the minority of Louis XIV. The Fronde (the name for the "sling" of a children's game played in the streets of Paris in defiance of civil authorities) was in part an attempt to check the growing power of royal government; its failure prepared the way for the absolutism of Louis XIV's personal reign.

The Fronde was a reaction to the policies begun under the Cardinal de Richelieu, chief minister of Louis XIII from 1624 to 1642, who weakened the influence of the nobility and reduced the powers of the judicial bodies, called Parlements. Opposition to the government from these privileged groups gained momentum from 1643 under the "foreign" rule of the queen regent Anne of Austria (Louis XIV's mother) and her Italian-born chief minister, Jules Cardinal Mazarin.

The refusal of the Parlement of Paris to approve the government's revenue measures in the spring of 1648 set off the first phase, the Fronde of the Parlement. The Parlement sought to put a constitutional limit on the monarchy by establishing its power to discuss and modify royal decrees. From June 30 to July 12 an assembly of courts made a list of 27 articles for reform, including abolition of the intendants (officials of the central government in the provinces), tax reductions, approval of all new taxes by the Parlement, and an end to arbitrary imprisonment. On July 31, Mazarin's government—at war with Spain—reluctantly agreed to many of the demands. With news of a victory over the Spanish, however, Anne and Mazarin felt strong enough to arrest two outspoken *parlementaires* on August 26, but an uprising in Paris forced the queen and her minister to release them two days later.

The conflict broke into war in January 1649. A blockade of Paris was not enough to force the surrender of the Parlement, which was supported by Parisian leaders and by some of the high nobility. Faced with disturbances in the provinces and the continuing foreign war, the government negotiated the Peace of Rueil (ratified April 1, 1649), which granted amnesty to the rebels and confirmed the concessions to Parlement.

The Fronde of the Princes, the second phase of the civil war (January 1650 to September 1653), was a complex of intrigues, rivalries, and shifts of allegiance in which constitutional issues gave way to personal ambitions. One common factor among the aristocratic rebels was opposition to Mazarin, who, throughout the Fronde, was the target of fierce attacks by pamphleteers. The Great Condé, a great military leader and cousin of the king, had helped the government in the war against the Parlement. Disappointed in his hope for political power, he became rebellious. When he was arrested, on January 18, 1650, his friends took up arms in a series of uprisings in the provinces, called the first war of the princes. By the end of 1650 the government had dealt successfully with the revolts. In reaction, the supporters of Condé and the Parisian party (sometimes called the Old Fronde) united to bring about the release of Condé and the dismissal of Mazarin (February 1651). Condé was dominant for a brief period.

Anne, however, knew how to exploit the divisions among the Frondeurs. She joined with the Old Fronde and ordered an indictment of Condé in August 1651, an act that decided Condé on war—the second war of the princes (September 1651 to September 1653). A main event of the war was Condé's entrance into Paris in April 1652. Despite Spanish aid, his position soon weakened: he was almost defeated by royal troops outside the walls of Paris (July 2, 1652), lost the support of the Parisian bourgeoisie, and never gained the approval of the Parlement. In the face of opposition, Condé left Paris on October 13 and eventually fled to the Spanish Netherlands. The king entered Paris in triumph on October 21, 1652, followed by Mazarin on February 3, 1653. With many of the nobles in exile and with the Parlement forbidden to interfere in royal administration, the Fronde ended in a clear victory for Mazarin.

Louis II de Bourbon (the Great Condé) rides his white horse to victory in the Battle of Lens (1648). The battle was one of the final conflicts of the Thirty Years' War.

its efforts to perpetuating the war in Germany. Although Mazarin had already signed a preliminary agreement with the emperor in September 1646, which conveyed parts of Alsace and Lorraine to France, in 1647–48 he started a new campaign in Germany in order to secure more. On May 17, 1648, another Bavarian army was destroyed at Zusmarshausen, near Nördlingen, and Maximilian's lands were occupied by the French.

Mazarin's desire to keep on fighting was thwarted by two developments. On the one hand, the pressure of the war on French taxpayers created tensions that in June 1648 erupted into the revolt known as the Fronde. On the other hand, Sweden made a separate peace with the emperor. The Stockholm government, still directed by Oxenstierna, was offered half of Pomerania, most of Mecklenburg, and the secularized bishoprics of Bremen and Verden; it was to receive a seat in the Imperial Diet; and the territories of the empire promised to pay five million thalers to the Swedish army for its wage arrears. With so many tangible gains, and with Germany so weakened that there was no risk of any further imperial attack, it was clearly time to wriggle out of the war, even without France. Peace was thus signed on August 6.

Without Sweden, Mazarin realized that France needed to make peace at the earliest opportunity. He settled with the emperor on easy terms: France gained only the transfer of a bundle of rights and territories in Alsace and Lorraine and little else. Mazarin could, nevertheless, derive satisfaction from the fact that the emperor was firmly excluded from the empire and was under oath to provide no further aid to Spain. The final treaty was signed on October 24, 1648. Mazarin settled down to suppress the Fronde revolt and to win the war against Philip IV.

PROBLEMS NOT SOLVED BY THE WAR

Some historians have sought to diminish the achievements of the Thirty Years' War, and the peace that ended it, because not all of Europe's outstanding problems were settled. It is true that the struggle between France and Spain continued with unabated bitterness until 1659. Within a decade of the Westphalian settlement, Sweden was at war with Poland (1655–60), Russia (1656–58), and Denmark (1657–58).

Many pieces of territory changed hands as a result of the Peace of Westphalia in 1648. The map also shows the boundary of the Holy Roman Empire after the treaty was signed.

In the east, a war broke out in 1654 between Poland and Russia that was to last until 1667, while tension between the Habsburgs and the Turks increased until war came in 1663. Even within the empire, there were disputes over the partition of Cleves-Jülich, still a battle zone after almost a half-century, which caused minor hostilities in 1651. Lorraine remained a theatre of war until the duke signed a final peace with France in 1661.

But a single conflict in early modern times could not have solved all of Europe's problems because the continent was not the single political system that it later became. Examined more closely, the peace conference that ended the Thirty Years' War settled a remarkable number of crucial issues.

PROBLEMS SOLVED BY THE WAR

The Congress of Westphalia was the beginning of a new order in Europe. The system depended on channeling the aggression of German princes from thoughts of conquering their neighbours to dreams of weakening them. It proved so successful that, for more than a century, the settlement of 1648 was widely regarded as the principal guarantee of order and peace in central Europe. The balance of power with its hinge in Germany, created by the Thirty Years' War and prolonged by the Peace of Westphalia, was a major achievement.

It was, for example, almost a century before German rulers went to war with each other again—a strong contrast with the hundred years before 1618, which had been full of armed neutrality and actual conflict. The reason for the contrast was simple: the Thirty Years' War had settled both of the crises that had so disturbed the peace in the decades before it began.

In the lands of the Austrian Habsburgs, there were now no powerful estates and no Protestant worship (except in Hungary), and, despite all the efforts of the Swedish diplomats at Westphalia, there was no restoration of the lands confiscated from rebels and others. The Habsburg

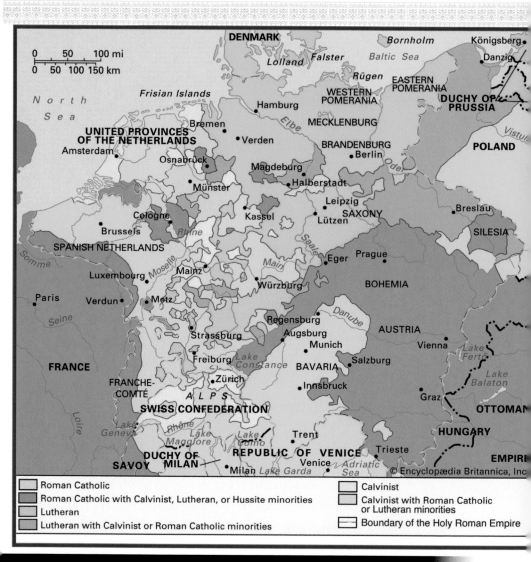

Roman Catholic
Roman Catholic with Calvinist, Lutheran, or Hussite minorities
Lutheran
Lutheran with Calvinist or Roman Catholic minorities

Calvinist
Calvinist with Roman Catholic
or Lutheran minorities
Boundary of the Holy Roman Empire

As a result of the Thirty Years' War, Germany in 1650 was made up of people of many different religious confessions, many of whom lived in close proximity to one another.

Monarchy, born of disparate units but now entirely under the authority of the king-emperor, had become a powerful state in its own right. Purged of political and religious dissidents and cut off from its western neighbours and from Spain, the compact private territories of the Holy Roman emperor were still large enough to guarantee him a place among the foremost rulers of Europe.

In the empire, by contrast, the new stability rested upon division rather than unity. Although the territorial rulers had acquired, at Westphalia, supreme power in their localities and collective power in the Diet to regulate common taxation, defense, laws, and public affairs without imperial intervention, the "amicable composition" formula prevented in fact any changes being made to the status quo. The originality of this compromise (enshrined in Article V, paragraph 52, of the Instrumentum Pacis Osnabrugense) has not always been appreciated. An age that normally revered the majority principle sanctioned an alternative method—parity between two unequal groups (known as *itio in partes*)—for reaching decisions.

Looked at more pragmatically, what the *itio in partes* formula achieved was to remove religion as a likely precipitant of political conflict. Although religion remained a matter of high political importance (for instance, in cementing an alliance against Louis XIV after 1685 or in unseating James II of England in 1688), it no longer determined international relations as it once had done.

Without question, those German princes who took up arms against Ferdinand II were strongly influenced by confessional considerations, and, as long as these men dominated the anti-Habsburg cause, so too did the issue of religion. Frederick of the Palatine and Christian of Anhalt, however, failed to secure a lasting settlement. Gradually the task of defending the Protestant cause fell into the hands of

Lutherans, less militant and less intransigent than the Calvinists. The Lutherans were prepared to ally, if necessary, with Anglican England, Catholic France, and even Orthodox Russia in order to create a coalition capable of defeating the Habsburgs. Naturally such states had their own reasons for fighting; and, although upholding the Protestant cause may have been among them, it seldom predominated.

After 1625, therefore, the role of religious issues in European politics steadily receded. This was, perhaps, the greatest achievement of the war. It eliminated the major destabilizing influence in European politics, which had both undermined the internal cohesion of many states and overturned the diplomatic balance of power created during the Renaissance.

Conclusion

uring the 16th century, Europe had transformed dramatically as a result of increased trade and production of goods, the establishment of new nation-states, and the Reformation and Counter-Reformation. These new economic, political, and religious conditions led to decades of war that radically changed the balance of power in Europe. Spain had lost not only the Netherlands but also its dominant position in western Europe. France was now the chief Western power. Sweden had control of the Baltic. The United Netherlands was recognized as an independent republic. The member states of the Holy Roman Empire were granted full sovereignty. The ancient notion of a Roman Catholic empire of Europe, headed spiritually by a pope and temporally by an emperor, was permanently abandoned, and the essential structure of modern Europe as a community of sovereign states was established.

Glossary

BALANCE OF POWER An equilibrium or adjustment of power (as between potentially opposing sovereign states) such that no one state is willing or able to upset the equilibrium by waging war or interfering with the independence of other states.

BOURGEOIS Of, belonging to, or characteristic of the social middle class.

CALVINISM The theology advanced by John Calvin, a Protestant Reformer in the 16th century, and its development by his followers. These theological doctrines emphasize the sovereignty of God in the bestowal of grace. Specifically, they include election or predestination, limited atonement, total depravity, irresistibility of grace, and the perseverance of saints.

CAPITAL Any accumulated factors of production capable of being owned.

CONCILIAR Of, relating to, or issued by a council.

CONFESSIONAL Adhering to, established on, or defined by a confession of faith.

CORSAIR A pirate.

CUIUS REGIO, EIUS RELIGIO A Latin phrase meaning "whose realm, his religion" that refers to the policy by which a population had to adhere to the faith (Catholic, Lutheran, etc.) of the ruler of that region.

DEMESNE An estate or land retained for the owner's own use.

ECCLESIASTICAL Of or relating to a church, especially as a formal and established institution.

FEUDAL Of, relating to, or having the characteristics of a feud or fief: founded upon or involving the relation of lord and vassal with tenure of land.

FOODSTUFFS The raw material of food before or after processing.

INFLATION An increase in the volume of money and credit relative to available goods resulting in a substantial and continuing rise in the general price level.

INTRANSIGENT Refusing to compromise or budge from an often extreme position taken or held; preserving an immovable independence of position or attitude.

LUTHERANISM The branch of Christianity that traces its interpretation of the Christian religion to the teachings of Martin Luther and the 16th-century movements that issued from his reforms. These teachings include the repudiation of papal and ecclesiastical authority in favour of the Bible, the rejection of five of the traditional seven sacraments affirmed by the Roman Catholic church, and the insistence that human reconciliation with God is effected solely by divine grace.

PERVASIVE Spread or spreading throughout all parts of something.

PRIMOGENITURE An exclusive right of inheritance; a right belonging under English law to the eldest son to take all the real estate of which an ancestor died.

PROTOINDUSTRIALIZATION A system of industrial organization that emerged in the 16th century and preceded industrialization, in which rural residents participated in craft production and an entrepreneur marketed the final products.

REMUNERATIVE Profitable or gainful.

SECULAR Of or relating to the worldly or temporal as distinguished from the spiritual or eternal; not sacred.

Bibliography

ECONOMY AND SOCIETY

The economic background of modern Europe is discussed in a variety of studies. Carlo M. Cipolla, *Before the Industrial Revolution: European Society and Economy, 1000–1700*, 2nd ed. (1980; originally published in Italian, 1974), offers a treatment of the economy focusing not so much on history as on social structures. Immanuel Wallerstein, *The Modern World-System*, 3 vol. (1974–89), covers the period from the 16th to the mid-19th century, emphasizing spatial division of the early capitalistic world among core areas, semiperipheries, and peripheries. Another broad, rich, and learned reconstruction of the world of early capitalism is offered in Fernand Braudel, *Civilization and Capitalism, 15th–18th Century*, 3 vol. (1982–84; originally published in French, 1979).

Comprehensive works include Rondo Cameron, *A Concise Economic History of the World: From Paleolithic Times to the Present* (1989); Harry A. Miskimin, *The Economy of Later Renaissance Europe, 1460–1600* (1977), stressing concepts of law as a critical factor in economic development; E.E. Rich and C.H. Wilson (eds.), *The Economy of Expanding Europe in the Sixteenth and Seventeenth Centuries* (1967); Jan De Vries, *Economy of Europe in an Age of Crisis, 1600–1750* (1976), exploring the 17th-century unraveling of the 16th-century world, and *European Urbanization, 1500–1800* (1984), a broader survey; Witold Kula, *An Economic Theory of the Feudal System: Towards a Model of the Polish Economy, 1500–1800*, new ed. (1976, reissued 1987; originally published in Polish, 1962), an analysis of a particular 16th-century economy; and Piero Camporesi, *Bread of*

Dreams: Food and Fantasy in Early Modern Europe (1989; originally published in Italian, 1980), an exploration of malnutrition with an impressive picture of some unpalatable food and the symbolism of its consumption.

Important demographic studies are Josiah Cox Russell, *The Control of Late Ancient and Medieval Population* (1985), a historical study of European communities; and E.A. Wrigley and R.S. Schofield, *The Population History of England, 1541–1871: A Reconstruction* (1981), utilizing new techniques of reconstruction and backward projection of census data.

Studies of protoindustrialization include Peter Kriedte et al., *Industrialization Before Industrialization: Rural Industry in the Genesis of Capitalism* (1981; originally published in German, 1977), in a German context; John U. Nef, *Industry and Government in France and England, 1540–1640* (1940, reprinted 1968), still informative and focusing on the interaction of power; and Paul Sweezy et al., *The Transition from Feudalism to Capitalism* (1976), a collection of Marxist debates as to what capitalism really was and when it began.

Matters concerning finance are studied in Earl J. Hamilton, *American Treasure and the Price Revolution in Spain, 1501–1650* (1934, reprinted 1977), a classic that launched a continuing debate. Political and cultural influences are the subject of Perry Anderson, *Lineages of the Absolutist State* (1974), a Marxist view of the role of the state in the birth of modern capitalism; Simon Schama, *The Embarrassment of Riches: An Interpretation of Dutch Culture in the Golden Age* (1987), a lengthy and entertaining exploration; Keith Thomas, *Religion and the Decline of Magic* (1971), on the impact of the culture of Reformation; and R.H. Tawney, *Religion and the Rise of Capitalism* (1926, reissued 1984), a classic study of Calvinism and the capitalistic ethos.

A broader approach to early modern society is offered summarily in Peter Burke, *The Historical Anthropology of Early Modern Italy: Essays on Perception and Communication* (1987), focusing on detail rather than central movements of early modern culture; Roger Chartier (ed.), *Passions of the Renaissance* (1989; originally published in French, 1986), a volume of essays dealing with the period from the Renaissance to Enlightenment, from the series *A History of Private Life*; Brian Pullan, *The Jews of Europe and the Inquisition of Venice, 1550–1670* (1983), an often poignant examination of ethnic relations; and Carlo Ginzburg, *The Cheese and the Worms: The Cosmos of a Sixteenth-Century Miller* (1980; originally published in Italian, 1976), an excellent social history based on the story of an eccentric miller and his cosmological views.

POLITICS AND DIPLOMACY

Politics and diplomacy are dealt with in many general histories of the period. Narrative and analytical accounts, with detailed bibliographies, are offered in J.R. Hale, *Renaissance Europe, 1480–1520* (1971, reprinted 1985); G.R. Elton, *Reformation Europe, 1517–1559* (1963); J.H. Elliott, *Europe Divided, 1559–1598* (1968, reprinted 1985); and Geoffrey Parker, *Europe in Crisis, 1598–1648* (1979), all four in the *Fontana History of Europe* series. G.R. Potter (ed.), *The Renaissance, 1493–1520* (1957); G.R. Elton (ed.), *The Reformation, 1520–1559*, 2nd ed. (1990); R.B. Wernham (ed.), *The Counter-Reformation and Price Revolution, 1559–1610* (1968); and J.P. Cooper (ed.), *The Decline of Spain and the Thirty Years War, 1609–48/59* (1970), the first four volumes in *The New Cambridge Modern History* series, offer a sequence of chapters by various authors, thematically organized. H.G. Koenigsberger, George L. Mosse, and G.Q. Bowler, *Europe in the Sixteenth Century*, 2nd ed. (1989), treats the earlier part of the period. The last 50 years of the period, dominated by the genesis and course of continental war, are best approached through Geoffrey Parker (ed.), *The Thirty Years' War*, rev. ed. (1987).

THE REFORMATION

General works on the history of Protestantism include Kenneth Scott Latourette, *A History of Christianity*, rev. ed., 2 vol. (1975), with useful bibliographies; and Émile G. Léonard, *A History of Protestantism* (1965–68; originally published in French in 3 vol., 1961–64).

Useful introductions to the late medieval and Reformation period are Thomas A. Brady, Heiko A. Oberman, and James D. Tracy (eds.), *Handbook of European History, 1400–1600: Late Middle Ages, Renaissance, and Reformation*, 2 vol. (1994–95); Hans J. Hillerbrand (ed.), *The Oxford Encyclopedia of the Reformation*, 4 vol. (1996); Heiko A. Oberman, *The Dawn of the Reformation: Essays in Late Medieval and Early Reformation Thought* (1986, reissued 1992); Francis Oakley, *The Western Church in the Later Middle Ages* (1979, reissued 1985); Steven Ozment, *The Age of Reform (1250–1550): An Intellectual and Religious History of Late Medieval and Reformation Europe* (1980); and Lewis W. Spitz, *The Protestant Reformation, 1517–1559* (1985, reissued 1987).

Among the more important studies of Martin Luther are Roland D.H. Bainton, *Here I Stand: A Life of Martin Luther* (1950, reissued 1995); Erik H. Erikson, *Young Man Luther: A Study in Psychoanalysis and History* (1958, reissued 1993); and

Heiko A. Oberman, *Luther: Man Between God and the Devil* (1989, reissued 1993; originally published in German, 1982). Good introductions to the life and influence of John Calvin are William J. Bouwsma, *John Calvin: A Sixteenth Century Portrait* (1988); and Alister E. McGrath, *A Life of John Calvin: A Study in the Shaping of Western Culture* (1990, reissued 1996).

Index